LEADERSHIP MASTERY

Mastering Strategy for Visionary Mindset

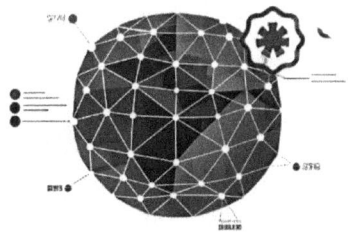

Dr. JORDAN Dickson

"The mark of lasting leadership isn't the number of battles won, but the legacy of wisdom, courage, and growth left in the hearts of those who followed."

Copyright © 2024 – Jordan Dickson

All rights to this book are reserved. No permission is given for any part of this book to be reproduced, transmitted in any form or means; electronic or mechanical, stored in a retrieval system, photocopied, recorded, scanned, or otherwise. Any of these actions require the proper written permission of the author.

DISCLAIMER

The information contained in this book is provided for educational and informational purposes only. The content is based on the author's personal experience and research and is not intended to serve as professional advice. Readers are encouraged to seek professional counsel relevant to their own specific circumstances.

The author and publisher disclaim any liability for any direct or indirect consequences arising from the use or application of the material in this book. All examples and scenarios mentioned are illustrative and should not be assumed to guarantee similar results.

Table of Contents

Preface	6
introduction	7
Part I: Foundations of Leadership Mastery	**9**
Chapter 1: The Power of Purpose	**1**
Defining Your "Why"	2
Visionary Leadership	3
Aligning Purpose with Action	5
Chapter 2: The Art of Strategic Thinking	**7**
Diagnosing Challenges and Opportunities	8
Setting Clear, Coherent Objectives	9
The Importance of Long-Term Thinking	10
Chapter 3: Competitive Advantage In A Challenging World	**13**
Understanding the Five Forces	13
Innovating in Deep Blue Strategy	15
Finding Your Niche: Playing to Win	16
Part II: Building and Leading High-Performing Teams	**18**
Chapter 4: Leadership that inspire Thoughts	**19**
Servant Leadership: Putting Others First	19
The Function of Vulnerability in Development of Trust	20
Leading by Example: The Ethics of Leadership	21
Chapter 5: Overcoming Team Dysfunctions	**23**
Building Trust and Embracing Conflict	23
Creating Commitment and Accountability	24
Driving Results through Team Synergy	25
Chapter 6: The Science of Motivation	**29**
Moving Beyond Carrot and Stick	29
Equipping Teams with Autonomy, Mastery, and Vision	30
Fostering a Culture of Continuous Growth	31

Part III: Strategic Tools for Success — 34
Chapter 7: The Strategic Playbook — 35
Applying Game Theory to Business Strategy: Thinking Like a Strategist — 35

Mastering Competitive Strategy and Execution: Moving Beyond Theory — 37

Decision-Making in Uncertain Times: Playing the Long Game — 38

Chapter 8: Data-driven Leadership — 41
Leveraging Metrics and Analytics for Informed Decisions — 41

Turning Insights into Action — 42

Tracking Progress for Continuous Improvement — 43

Empowering Data-Driven Leadership — 44

Chapter 9: Creating uncontested markets — 45
Identifying Blue Oceans and Opportunities — 45

Differentiating Through Innovation — 46

Scaling Sustainable Success — 47

Part IV: Personal Development and Resilience — 50
Chapter 10: The Beauty of Imperfection — 51
Embracing Vulnerability for Personal Growth — 51

Overcoming Fear and Shame in Leadership — 52

Nurturing Courage, Compassion, and Connection — 52

Chapter 11: The leader's Growth mindset — 55
Lifelong Learning — 56

Resilience and Self-care — 57

Chapter 12: Finding Meaning In Leadership — 59
Leading with Purpose Beyond Profit — 59

Seeking Answers To Life's Big Questions — 61

The Legacy of a Leader: Impact and Significance — 62

Chapter 13: Practical Management for Leadership Mastery — 65
Balancing Empathy, Execution, and Growth — 65

Empathy as a Strategic Tool — 65

Table of Contents

The Power of Clear Communication	66
Execution: Turning Vision into Reality	67
Fostering Growth and Development	68
Leaving a Lasting Legacy	69

Part V: Achieving Greatness — **71**

Chapter 14: From Good to great: The Path to sustained success — **73**

Developing Level 5 Leadership	73
Building a Hedgehog Concept: Passion, Skill, and Value	74
The Flywheel and the Doom Loop: Momentum vs. Stagnation	75
Practical Application and Final Thoughts	77

Chapter 15: Strategic Execution: Turning Plans into Action — **79**

Closing the Distance Between Strategy and Execution	79
Continuous Adaptation and Flexibility in Leadership	80
Measuring Success and Learning from Failure	81
Strategic Execution in Practice	82

Chapter 16: leading into the future — **85**

Future-Proofing Your Strategy	85
Adapting to Technological and Cultural Shifts	86
Leaving a Lasting Impact: The Role of Legacy in Leadership	87
Leadership Beyond the Present	89

Conclusion — **90**

Appendix	91
Practical Tools and Worksheets for Strategic Planning	91
About the Author	101
Index	103

Preface

In an era where change is constant and challenges are inevitable, leadership requires more than simply responding to the moment—it demands foresight, adaptability, and a deep understanding of strategy. Leadership Mastery is not just another book on leadership; it's a comprehensive guide for leaders who aspire to do more than manage. It's for those who seek to transform their vision into reality, drive sustainable growth, and leave a lasting legacy.

Through years of working with leaders across various industries, I have observed one undeniable truth: the most successful leaders are those who possess a strategic mindset. They don't just react to the present; they anticipate the future, craft visionary strategies, and empower their teams to succeed. In this book, I share actionable insights and proven strategies that will help you develop the mindset necessary to lead with intention, clarity, and purpose.

Whether you're a seasoned leader or just beginning your journey, Strategic Leadership Mindset will equip you with the tools to navigate complexity, inspire your team, and achieve long-term success. Let this book be your guide to becoming the leader you were meant to be—one who shapes the future rather than merely responding to it.

— Dr. Jordan Dickson

INTRODUCTION

Leadership is not just about holding a position of power or setting High-level objectives. It's about shaping your thinking to navigate through uncertainty, adapt to changing environments, and inspire others to do the same. At its core, leadership is a mindset. A Strategic Leadership Mindset is what separates those who merely react from those who shape the future.

As Sun Tzu famously said, "Strategy without tactics is the slowest route to victory. Tactics without strategy is the noise before defeat." This truth holds more relevance today than ever before. In a world of rapid change, the leaders who thrive are those who understand that strategy and mindset go hand in hand.

Let me share a quick story to illustrate. A few years ago, I had a conversation with an entrepreneur who had started a tech company that was skyrocketing to success. But as is often the case, the honeymoon phase ended abruptly when a well-funded competitor entered the market. Panic ensued within the company, employees started questioning their future, and even the entrepreneur himself began doubting his vision. Instead of trying to outspend his competition or react hastily, he shifted his focus to something deeper—his mindset. He revisited his core purpose, reevaluated his strengths, and redefined his strategy. Within a few months, his company launched an innovative product that his competitor couldn't replicate, and they regained their momentum. They didn't just survive the competition—they dominated.

This story illustrates a key point: The strength of your leadership isn't just in your skills or knowledge, but in how you think. This book is about helping you cultivate a Leadership Mastery, one that empowers you to make confident decisions, drive growth, and build a lasting legacy.

What does this mindset look like? It's about being visionary yet grounded in reality. It's about balancing analytical thinking with creativity. It's about leading with authenticity, making tough choices with clarity, and turning obstacles into opportunities. Whether you're leading a startup, managing a team, or running a large organization, the ability to think strategically will be the key to your success.

This book will provide you with the insights, tools, and techniques to do just that. You'll learn how to:

- Identify and seize opportunities, even when the odds seem against you.
- Develop a clear and compelling vision, and align your team around it.
- Make decisions with confidence, balancing short-term wins with long-term success.
- Inspire your team by leading with authenticity and purpose.
- Cultivate resilience, allowing you to adapt and thrive through uncertainty.

Ultimately, this book is about transformation. It's about equipping you with the mindset needed to elevate your leadership and navigate whatever challenges come your way. Every chapter is filled with practical strategies, real-life examples, and thought-provoking exercises designed to help you grow as a leader.

So, are you ready to unlock your potential? Let's embark on this journey together, and build a mindset that will not only survive but shape the future of leadership.

Introduction

DR. JORDAN DICKSON

Leadership Mastery

Part I: Foundations of Leadership Mastery

CHAPTER 1: THE POWER OF PURPOSE

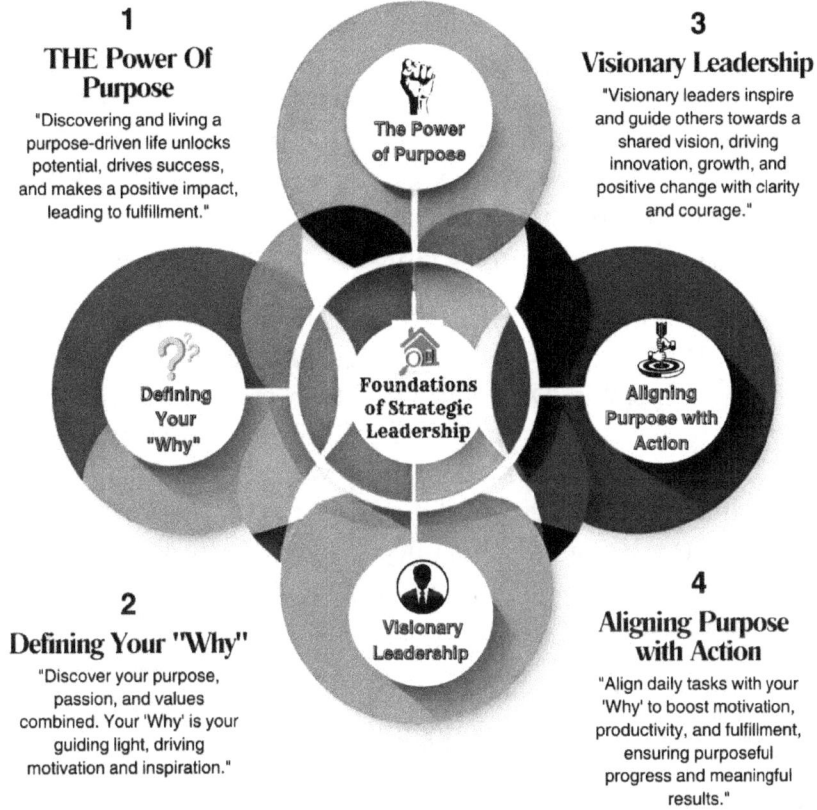

Leadership is much more than just holding a title or being in charge. It's about knowing why you do what you do and leading with a deep sense of purpose. When we talk about a Leadership Mastery, it all begins with that foundation—purpose. Without purpose, leadership becomes aimless, reactive, and easily swayed by short-term pressures. But with purpose, leadership becomes intentional, decisive, and, most importantly, powerful.

Let me take you through a few real-life examples of how purpose-driven leadership has created lasting success, and why understanding your own "why" is the first step toward becoming a truly strategic leader.

Defining Your "Why"

Michael, a healthcare executive, spent years driving his company toward success. Under his leadership, the business grew, increased market share, and hit profitability targets. But despite all the outward signs of success, Michael felt an inner disconnect. The decisions he made were profitable in the short term but left him questioning whether his company was staying true to its deeper mission: improving patient lives through ethical healthcare practices.

The turning point for Michael came during a major ethical dilemma. His company was presented with a choice—continue a lucrative partnership with a vendor that was cutting corners on patient care or cut ties and face significant short-term financial losses. The easy choice was clear—stay with the vendor, protect the bottom line, and preserve profitability. But Michael couldn't shake the feeling that something was deeply wrong with that decision. It was in that moment of moral tension that Michael reconnected with his purpose.

His "why" wasn't about financial success—it was about ensuring that his company lived up to its promise of ethical care. Instead of taking the easier, more profitable route, Michael made the tougher choice to walk away from the partnership. At first, the decision caused financial strain, and some stakeholders questioned the wisdom of his choice. But in the long run, Michael's decision paid off in ways he never imagined. The company's reputation soared, patient trust grew, and soon, new opportunities for growth emerged—ones that aligned with Michael's purpose of ethical healthcare.

What made this possible wasn't just the act of making a tough decision—it was the fact that Michael had reconnected with his core purpose and allowed it to guide his leadership.

Howard Schultz of Starbucks is another brilliant example of a leader driven by purpose. Schultz didn't just want to sell coffee; he envisioned Starbucks as a "third place" between home and work, a space where people could gather, connect, and build community. Schultz's "why" was rooted in creating connection and belonging. His purpose went beyond profits—it was about building relationships, fostering community, and offering customers a personal experience.

This purpose shaped every aspect of Starbucks—from the way stores were designed, to how employees were treated, to the company's expansion strategy. When Starbucks faced tough times, particularly during the economic downturn of 2008, Schultz returned as CEO with the sole aim of reconnecting the company to its original purpose. He closed hundreds of stores, overhauled operations, and reemphasized quality over quantity. His actions were guided by his purpose, not by immediate financial gain. In the end, his decision to refocus on Starbucks' core values helped the company recover, thrive, and grow even stronger.

> *His "why" wasn't about financial success—it was about ensuring that his company lived up to its promise of ethical care.*

What Schultz shows us is that when your purpose is clear, it serves as a guiding principle during difficult decisions. It's not just about profits or market share—it's about creating something bigger, something meaningful.

VISIONARY LEADERSHIP

Purpose by itself isn't enough. Once you've defined your "why," the next step is to craft a vision that aligns with it. Visionary leadership is about taking your purpose and transforming it into a clear, actionable, and inspiring future. It's not just about having a vague idea of where you want to go, but about having a precise direction that drives every decision and action.

Consider Elon Musk, one of the most visionary leaders of our time. Musk's purpose is clear: to advance humanity through technology. But it's his vision—one that aligns perfectly with his purpose—that has captured the world's imagination. Musk doesn't just see himself as running companies like Tesla or SpaceX—he envisions a future where humanity is no longer bound to Earth, where sustainable energy powers our lives, and where technology solves our most pressing problems.

Musk's vision is bold and seemingly impossible to many. Colonizing Mars? Building electric vehicles that outperform gas-powered cars? These are ideas that most would write off as dreams. But what makes Musk's leadership so powerful is that his vision is rooted in a deep, personal purpose. He truly believes that his work can push humanity forward, and that belief drives his relentless pursuit of innovation.

One of the key moments in Musk's journey came with the near-collapse of both Tesla and SpaceX. At one point, Musk had to decide which of his companies to save with his dwindling resources. His vision guided him through that difficult period, and instead of abandoning one, he doubled down on both. Musk's commitment to his vision, despite overwhelming odds, led to the eventual success of both companies. Today, Tesla is a global leader in electric vehicles, and SpaceX is pioneering the future of space travel.

Visionary leadership isn't just for CEOs like Musk. Whether you're leading a small team, running a startup, or managing a large corporation, having a clear vision that aligns with your purpose is critical. Vision gives you and your team a sense of direction and meaning. It turns ordinary tasks into part of a larger mission.

When you lead with a vision that's deeply connected to your purpose, you inspire others to believe in what you're doing and to join you in making that vision a reality.

ALIGNING PURPOSE WITH ACTION

Having a purpose and vision is essential, but purpose alone won't create impact unless it's backed by consistent, aligned action. One of the most common mistakes leaders make is failing to bridge the gap between what they believe in and what they do. Without alignment between purpose and action, leaders lose credibility, teams lose focus, and results suffer.

Indra Nooyi, the former CEO of PepsiCo, offers a powerful example of what it means to align purpose with action. Nooyi had a clear purpose for PepsiCo: to make the company a global leader in health and sustainability. But she didn't stop at a high-level vision. She took concrete steps to transform the company's product lines, reduce its environmental impact, and reshape its entire culture to align with her purpose.

Nooyi's decision to shift PepsiCo's focus toward healthier products was not an easy one. It required significant investment in research and development, changes to the supply chain, and a long-term commitment to sustainability. Many questioned whether these moves were wise, given the immediate pressure for financial returns. However, Nooyi's purpose-driven approach was clear: the future of the company depended on aligning with consumer demands for healthier, more sustainable options. Over time, PepsiCo became a leader in promoting health and wellness in the food and beverage industry. Nooyi's actions—consistent with her purpose—helped build trust with consumers, employees, and investors alike. Her leadership demonstrated that when purpose and action are aligned, the impact is far-reaching and sustainable.

Aligning purpose with action requires discipline, clarity, and sometimes making difficult decisions. But it's in these moments that leadership is truly tested. Leaders who act in alignment with their purpose build trust, foster loyalty, and create lasting impact.

Bringing It All Together

So, what do Michael, Howard Schultz, Elon Musk, and Indra Nooyi have in common? They all lead with a clear purpose, craft visionary futures aligned with that purpose, and take consistent, decisive action to bring that vision to life. They don't just react to external pressures—they lead from within, guided by their core values and beliefs.

For you, as a leader, the takeaway is this: Purpose is your anchor. It gives meaning to your work and helps you navigate even the most challenging decisions. But purpose alone isn't enough. You need to turn that purpose into a vision that inspires and guides your team. And then, you must take action—actions that align with your purpose and move you closer to your vision.

In the chapters that follow, we'll explore how you can develop this strategic leadership mindset. You'll learn how to identify opportunities, make informed decisions, and lead with authenticity and confidence. But remember, everything starts with purpose. It's the bedrock of great leadership and the foundation upon which everything else is built.By connecting with your purpose, crafting a compelling vision, and aligning your actions with your values, you will not only become a more effective leader but also build a legacy that stands the test of time.

Chapter 2: The Art of Strategic Thinking

In the fast-paced and ever-evolving world of leadership, strategic thinking is an art—a delicate balance of diagnosing challenges, identifying opportunities, setting clear objectives, and considering the long-term horizon. To develop a strategic leadership mindset, you need to sharpen your ability to think beyond the immediate. Strategic thinking is not about reacting to events as they come, but about proactively shaping the future.

One of the key traits that separates great leaders from average ones is their ability to think strategically. They are the ones who step back, assess the bigger picture, and map out a path to success. Strategic thinking enables you to move beyond the day-to-day grind, anticipate potential pitfalls, and seize emerging opportunities that others might miss. This chapter delves into the nuances of strategic thinking, offering insights from some of the most successful leaders, and practical tools to develop this critical skill.

Diagnosing Challenges and Opportunities

Effective strategic thinking starts with the ability to diagnose the situation at hand—understanding both the challenges and the opportunities. This diagnostic ability is crucial for setting a course of action that addresses the right issues while leveraging the best chances for success.

Take **Steve Jobs** for example. When Jobs returned to Apple in 1997, the company was on the verge of collapse, drowning in a sea of poorly performing products. Jobs didn't just focus on trimming costs or ramping up sales; he took a step back and diagnosed Apple's fundamental challenge: lack of focus. Apple had too many products, diluting its identity and overwhelming customers. Jobs' strategic response was to slash the product line, focus on just a handful of core products, and streamline the company's operations. This diagnosis—cutting away the excess to focus on innovation—set Apple on a trajectory that would eventually make it one of the most valuable companies in the world.

Jobs' ability to diagnose Apple's problem wasn't just based on financial data or market trends; it came from his deep understanding of the company's DNA and his intuition about what customers really wanted. Strategic thinking, like Jobs demonstrated, requires a blend of analytical insight and intuitive understanding.

But diagnosing challenges is only one side of the coin. Strategic leaders also need to be adept at identifying opportunities, often where others see only obstacles. **Howard Schultz** at Starbucks, after returning to the company as CEO, saw an opportunity in the economic downturn of 2008. While many companies were cutting back, Schultz invested in redesigning stores and enhancing the Starbucks experience. He focused on the emotional connection customers had with Starbucks, rather than just trying to sell coffee. Schultz's strategic thinking—rooted in seeing an opportunity to deepen customer loyalty even during tough times—enabled Starbucks to emerge stronger from the recession.

The ability to diagnose challenges and opportunities requires both analytical skills and a deep understanding of your organization's core strengths and weaknesses. It's about looking at the facts, interpreting them in context, and understanding how they fit into the bigger picture.

Setting Clear, Coherent Objectives

Once you've diagnosed the situation, the next step is setting clear and coherent objectives. Strategic leadership isn't just about identifying problems and opportunities—it's about charting a course of action that aligns with your long-term vision and purpose.

Clear objectives give your team a sense of direction. They help focus resources, energy, and attention on what truly matters. But setting objectives is an art in itself—it requires balancing ambition with feasibility, clarity with flexibility, and short-term needs with long-term goals.

One leader who excelled at setting clear, coherent objectives was **Jeff Bezos**. When Bezos founded Amazon, his long-term vision was to create the *"Everything Store"*—an online platform where customers could buy virtually anything they wanted. But Bezos didn't simply throw out this grand vision and leave his team to figure out how to get there. He set clear, incremental objectives that were coherent with his long-term strategy.

In the early days, Amazon focused exclusively on books. Bezos knew that starting small would allow Amazon to build the infrastructure, logistics, and brand necessary for future growth. Over time, as Amazon mastered each objective, Bezos expanded into new product categories, always keeping his broader vision in mind. The clarity and coherence of his objectives allowed Amazon to grow methodically and strategically, rather than trying to do everything at once.

Another example is **Indra Nooyi** at PepsiCo. When Nooyi became CEO, she set the objective of transforming PepsiCo into a leader in health and wellness. This was a radical shift for a company that had been primarily known for its sugary sodas and snacks. But Nooyi didn't simply declare the objective and hope for the best—she set clear, actionable goals for reformulating products, investing in healthier alternatives, and expanding PepsiCo's presence in the health-conscious market. Her objectives were not only ambitious but also coherent with her vision of a healthier, more sustainable future for PepsiCo.

The key takeaway here is that strategic leaders set objectives that are clear, actionable, and aligned with their long-term vision. These objectives provide a roadmap for decision-making and keep the organization focused on what matters most.

The Importance of Long-Term Thinking

One of the most significant differences between tactical and strategic thinking is the timeframe. Tactical thinking is about solving immediate problems and achieving short-term goals. Strategic thinking, on the other hand, is about positioning your organization for success over the long term. It's about anticipating future trends, preparing for potential disruptions, and building a sustainable competitive advantage.

Elon Musk is a master of long-term thinking. When Musk founded **SpaceX**His goal wasn't just to build rockets—it was to make humanity a multiplanetary species by colonizing Mars. This vision, though audacious, is what drives every decision Musk makes at

SpaceX. While other companies might focus on quarterly earnings or short-term contracts, Musk keeps his eye on the long-term goal of advancing space exploration and eventually colonizing Mars.

Musk's long-term thinking allows SpaceX to take risks that other companies might avoid. For example, SpaceX has invested heavily in reusable rocket technology—an innovation that has the potential to dramatically reduce the cost of space travel over time. While the upfront investment was enormous and the risk of failure high, Musk's long-term vision justified the decision. Today, SpaceX is leading the space industry in innovation, largely because of Musk's willingness to think beyond the immediate and plan for the future.

Long-term thinking isn't just about having a big vision—it's about making decisions today that position your organization for future success. **Warren Buffett** often talks about long-term thinking in terms of investing. Buffett doesn't make decisions based on short-term market fluctuations or quarterly earnings reports. Instead, he invests in companies that have strong fundamentals and long-term potential. Buffett's approach is grounded in patience, discipline, and a deep understanding of how businesses create value over time.

In leadership, long-term thinking is critical for creating sustainable success. It's easy to get caught up in the day-to-day demands of running a business or managing a team, but strategic leaders always keep one eye on the future. They make decisions with the long term in mind, even when it means sacrificing short-term gains.

Lessons from **Satya Nadella,** CEO of Microsoft. When Nadella took over, Microsoft was struggling to compete in a rapidly changing tech landscape. Rather than focus solely on immediate fixes, Nadella took a long-term approach, shifting Microsoft's focus to cloud computing and artificial intelligence—areas that would define the future of technology. This long-term strategy has revitalized Microsoft, transforming it from a company that seemed to be falling behind into a leader in innovation and growth.

By adopting a Strategic Leadership mindset like Satya Nadella's, leaders can Drive Transformation, innovation, and success in their organization.

Strategic thinking is at the heart of effective leadership. It's about diagnosing challenges and opportunities, setting clear and coherent objectives, and maintaining a focus on the long term. Leaders who master the art of strategic thinking are able to navigate uncertainty, seize opportunities, and position their organizations for lasting success.

The examples of **Steve Jobs, Howard Schultz, Jeff Bezos, Indra Nooyi, Elon Musk, Warren Buffett, and Satya Nadella** illustrate the power of strategic thinking in action. These leaders didn't just react to events—they anticipated them, set bold objectives, and made decisions with the future in mind.

As you develop your own strategic leadership mindset, remember that strategic thinking isn't just about having the right answers—it's about asking the right questions, thinking ahead, and staying true to your purpose and vision. It's about seeing beyond the present and crafting a future that aligns with your values and goals.

Chapter 3: Competitive Advantage In A Challenging World

The modern business landscape is constantly shifting, driven by technological advancements, globalization, and evolving consumer preferences. To succeed in this dynamic environment, leaders must focus on building and maintaining a competitive advantage. But what does competitive advantage look like today, in a world where disruption is the norm, and competition is fiercer than ever?

In this chapter, we'll explore the frameworks and strategies that can help you gain and sustain a competitive edge. Whether it's by understanding your competitive landscape, innovating in untapped markets, or finding your niche and playing to win, the principles of strategic leadership will guide you toward long-term success.

Understanding the Five Forces

The foundation of any strategic approach to competition lies in understanding the forces that shape your industry. Michael E. Porter, one of the foremost thinkers in competitive strategy, developed the concept of the Five Forces, which provides a framework for analyzing the competitive forces that influence profitability in any industry. Porter's Five Forces are:

1. The threat of new entrants: How easy is it for new competitors to enter your market? High barriers to entry, such as capital requirements or regulatory hurdles, can protect your competitive advantage.

2. The bargaining power of suppliers: How much power do suppliers have over your business? If you rely on a few key suppliers who can raise prices or limit supply, your competitive advantage may be at risk.

3. The bargaining power of buyers: Can your customers easily switch to a competitor? High buyer power can force businesses to lower prices, impacting profitability.

4. The threat of substitute products: Are there alternative products or services that can fulfill the same need as yours? A high threat of substitutes can reduce demand for your offerings.

5. The intensity of competitive rivalry: How fierce is the competition in your industry? High levels of competition can drive prices down and squeeze profit margins.

Take **Netflix,** for example. When Netflix first started its streaming service, it disrupted the traditional entertainment industry and changed the way people consumed media. But even Netflix is subject to Porter's Five Forces. The threat of new entrants is high, with competitors like Disney+, Amazon Prime, and Hulu constantly vying for market share. The bargaining power of suppliers (content creators and studios) is also strong, as they can choose to license their content to the highest bidder or launch their own streaming services. Netflix's response to these forces has been strategic: it invests heavily in original content, reducing its reliance on external suppliers, and continues to innovate in user experience and technology to maintain its competitive edge.

By understanding the Five Forces, leaders can better anticipate potential threats and opportunities in their industry and create strategies that strengthen their competitive position. Rather than reacting to external pressures, you can proactively shape the competitive landscape to your advantage.

INNOVATING IN DEEP BLUE STRATEGY

In a world of fierce competition, one of the most powerful strategies for gaining a competitive advantage is to move away from crowded, cutthroat markets—what **W. Chan Kim and Renée Mauborgne** call "red oceans"—and create new, uncontested market spaces, or "blue oceans." Deep Blue strategy is about innovation and differentiation. Rather than competing head-to-head with rivals, companies that successfully implement deep blue strategies create entirely new markets or reshape existing ones, making the competition irrelevant.

A classic example of blue ocean strategy is **Cirque du Soleil**. In a market dominated by traditional circuses with their reliance on animal acts and clowns, Cirque du Soleil redefined the circus experience by blending theatrical performance, music, and acrobatics. By appealing to a more sophisticated, adult audience and charging premium prices, Cirque du Soleil created a new market space where it had no direct competitors.

Another example is **Tesla**. When **Elon Musk** launched Tesla, he didn't just build another car company—he created an electric vehicle (EV) revolution. At the time, the auto industry was a red ocean of cutthroat competition, with major manufacturers competing on price, fuel efficiency, and brand loyalty. Tesla bypassed this traditional market by focusing on luxury electric vehicles with cutting-edge technology and design, carving out a blue ocean where it had little competition initially. Tesla's focus on innovation, design, and sustainability has since set it apart as a leader in the EV market.

Blue ocean strategy requires visionary thinking and the courage to step outside traditional industry boundaries. Leaders who can identify unmet customer needs, redefine the value proposition, and execute bold ideas are more likely to achieve sustainable competitive advantage.

Finding Your Niche: Playing to Win

While broad strategies like Porter's Five Forces and blue ocean strategy offer valuable insights, another approach to gaining a competitive advantage is finding your niche and "playing to win." This means understanding your unique strengths, identifying where you can win, and focusing your efforts on that area.

Roger L. Martin and A.G. Lafley, in their book **Playing to Win**, emphasize the importance of making deliberate choices about where and how to compete. Successful leaders don't try to be everything to everyone—they focus on winning in specific areas where they have a competitive edge.

Take **Nike**, for example. Nike's niche isn't just sportswear—it's about empowering athletes to achieve their best performance. Nike's **"Just Do It"** campaign wasn't just a slogan; it was a bold statement that resonated with athletes of all levels. By focusing on innovation in athletic performance, emotional branding, and partnerships with top athletes, Nike has maintained its position as a global leader in sports apparel and footwear. Nike didn't try to compete on price or with every possible demographic; instead, it focused on its niche and became synonymous with athletic excellence.

Similarly, **Southwest Airlines** found its niche by focusing on low-cost, no-frills air travel. Southwest didn't try to compete with major airlines on luxury or global routes. Instead, it honed in on its unique strengths—efficient operations, low-cost fares, and a fun, customer-centric culture—and dominated the domestic short-haul market. By playing to win in its specific niche, Southwest carved out a space where it could thrive.

Even in highly competitive markets, finding your niche and playing to your strengths can be a game-changer. **Patagonia** is another great example. Instead of competing with every outdoor apparel company, Patagonia focused on sustainability and environmental activism. Its commitment to ethical practices and environmentally friendly products has created a loyal customer base that shares its values. Patagonia's niche strategy has not only given it a competitive advantage but also allowed it to thrive as a purpose-driven brand.

In a changing world, gaining and maintaining a competitive advantage requires strategic thinking, innovation, and a clear sense of purpose. By understanding the competitive forces at play, leaders can better navigate challenges and seize opportunities. Innovating in blue oceans allows companies to escape the intense competition of red oceans and create new markets where they can thrive. And by finding their niche and playing to win, leaders can focus on their unique strengths and carve out a space where they can succeed.

The examples of *Netflix, Cirque du Soleil, Tesla, Nike, Southwest Airlines, and Patagonia* show that competitive advantage doesn't come from following the crowd—it comes from understanding the landscape, thinking creatively, and being bold enough to play to your strengths. Whether you're a startup or a seasoned business, these strategies will help you build a sustainable competitive advantage in today's ever-changing world.

DR. JORDAN DICKSON
Leadership Mastery

Part II: Building and Leading High-Performing Teams

CHAPTER 4: LEADERSHIP THAT INSPIRE THOUGHTS

In the heart of every successful team is a leader who inspires trust. Trust isn't built overnight; it requires consistency, empathy, and a willingness to be vulnerable. To cultivate a high-performing team, leaders must embody the values they wish to see in their team members, balancing authority with humility and decisiveness with empathy.

Leadership isn't just about giving orders or setting goals—it's about creating an environment where people feel safe, respected, and empowered to bring their best selves to work. In this chapter, we'll explore the key principles of leadership that inspire trust, focusing on servant leadership, vulnerability, and leading by example through ethical decision-making.

Servant Leadership: Putting Others First

At the core of building trust is the practice of servant leadership. This concept, first popularized by **Robert K. Greenleaf**, suggests that great leaders are those who serve their people first. Servant leaders prioritize the needs of their team, ensuring that individuals feel valued, heard, and supported. When leaders adopt a servant mindset, they flip the traditional power dynamic—rather than viewing leadership as control over others, it becomes a responsibility to elevate and empower the team.

A powerful example of servant leadership is **Howard Schultz**, the former CEO of Starbucks. Schultz's leadership style was deeply rooted in empathy and care for his employees, which he referred to as "partners." During his tenure, Schultz made it a priority to offer healthcare benefits to part-time employees, an uncommon practice in corporate America. He also created opportunities for career growth, education, and personal development within the company. Schultz's dedication to his team earned him the trust of his employees, fostering loyalty and a sense of shared purpose across the organization.

Effective leaders know that the success of those they oversee determines their own success.
By putting others first, leaders inspire trust and loyalty, which translates into higher levels of engagement, performance, and innovation within the team.

THE FUNCTION OF VULNERABILITY IN DEVELOPMENT OF TRUST

Many leaders believe that showing vulnerability is a sign of weakness. But in reality, vulnerability is one of the most powerful tools a leader can use to build trust. When leaders are open about their challenges, admit their mistakes, and share their fears, they create a culture of authenticity and psychological safety. Team members feel more comfortable being themselves, taking risks, and voicing their ideas.

One of the most influential voices on vulnerability is **Brené Brown**, whose research has shown that vulnerability is essential to building strong relationships. Vulnerable leaders demonstrate that it's okay to be imperfect and that mistakes are part of the journey. This authenticity makes leaders relatable and approachable, strengthening the bond between leader and team.

Consider **Elon Musk**, CEO of Tesla and SpaceX. Musk is known for being transparent about his struggles, including the very public challenges Tesla faced in ramping up production of its electric vehicles. Musk famously slept on the factory floor during Tesla's "production hell," showing his team that he was fully committed to solving the problem alongside them. By embracing vulnerability and sharing in the struggles of his company, Musk earned the trust and respect of his team. His example illustrates that vulnerability is not about oversharing, but about demonstrating a willingness to be open and authentic, even in difficult times.

When leaders embrace vulnerability, they foster an environment where team members feel safe to take risks and innovate. Trust grows in the space where people are allowed to be themselves without fear of judgment or reprisal.

LEADING BY EXAMPLE: THE ETHICS OF LEADERSHIP

Perhaps the most crucial aspect of trust-building in leadership is leading by example. The behaviors, values, and principles that leaders demonstrate set the standard for the rest of the team. Ethical leadership is about consistently acting with integrity, fairness, and honesty, even when faced with difficult decisions. Leaders who model ethical behavior earn the trust of their team, which in turn creates a culture of accountability and mutual respect.

Take the case of **Michael Josephson,** founder of the Josephson Institute of Ethics, who famously said, *"People will follow your actions, not your words."* Ethical leadership isn't about giving motivational speeches or sharing moral platitudes; it's about acting in ways that align with the values you preach. When leaders consistently act with integrity, they set the tone for the entire organization. Employees will follow suit, knowing that ethical behavior is not just expected but lived out by their leader.

Consider the example of **Satya Nadella,** CEO of Microsoft, who has gained widespread respect for his empathetic, values-driven leadership. Nadella's commitment to diversity and inclusion, as well as his emphasis on a growth mindset, has transformed Microsoft's culture. Under his leadership, the company shifted from a competitive, "know-it-all" mentality to a more collaborative, **"learn-it-all"** mindset. Nadella's approach is rooted in ethics and integrity—he not only preaches these values but embodies them in his leadership style. By leading with empathy and fairness, Nadella has earned the trust of both his employees and the broader industry, driving Microsoft to new heights of success.

Ethical leadership is about being consistent and fair in your actions, even when no one is watching. It's about making decisions that align with your values and holding yourself accountable to the same standards you expect from your team. When leaders lead by example, they cultivate trust and loyalty, building a strong foundation for high-performing teams.

Leadership that inspires trust is not built on authority or control—it's built on empathy, authenticity, and integrity. Servant leadership puts the needs of the team first, showing that leaders are there to serve rather than command. Vulnerability fosters a culture of openness and psychological safety, allowing teams to innovate and grow. Ethical leadership sets the standard for the organization, ensuring that trust is maintained through consistent and fair actions.

By embodying these principles, leaders can inspire the trust and loyalty of their teams, unlocking higher levels of engagement, performance, and innovation. High-performing teams are not just a result of smart strategy or tactical execution—they are a reflection of the trust that leaders cultivate through their actions, words, and values.

Chapter 5: Overcoming Team Dysfunctions

In any team, dysfunctions are inevitable. Even the most high-performing groups face obstacles—mistrust, lack of accountability, poor communication, and conflicting priorities can all erode performance. The difference between a mediocre team and an exceptional one lies in how these dysfunctions are identified and addressed. This chapter explores how leaders can effectively tackle common team dysfunctions by building trust, embracing conflict, fostering commitment, instilling accountability, and driving results through team synergy.

Building Trust and Embracing Conflict

Trust is the bedrock of any successful team. Without trust, collaboration becomes superficial, and dysfunction is almost guaranteed. Yet, trust is fragile and takes time to cultivate. In many cases, team dysfunctions arise when trust is lacking, leading to an environment where members feel guarded and defensive. To build trust, leaders must promote openness, vulnerability, and authenticity.

An excellent real-world example comes from **Ray Dalio,** founder of Bridgewater Associates, one of the world's largest hedge funds. Dalio implemented a culture of "radical transparency" where every meeting is recorded, and employees are encouraged to provide honest feedback, regardless of hierarchy. This approach breaks down barriers and encourages open, sometimes uncomfortable discussions. It forces team members to confront issues directly rather than allowing dysfunctions to fester beneath the surface.

Conflict is often viewed as negative, but when managed properly, it can actually strengthen teams. Embracing healthy conflict—where disagreements are addressed openly, and solutions are collaboratively forged—leads to better decision-making and more innovative solutions. This principle isn't limited to the corporate world; in **political leadership** leaders often thrive by leveraging conflict to bring diverse perspectives together. Take **Nelson Mandela**, who, instead of avoiding the deep racial conflict in post-apartheid South Africa, confronted it head-on. Mandela fostered reconciliation between groups that had been at odds for decades by creating forums for honest discussion and trust-building initiatives.

In the **social security** arena, particularly in public policy discussions, trust between politicians, the public, and institutions is crucial. When policymakers lack transparency or fail to engage stakeholders honestly, public distrust grows, which can lead to gridlock and stagnation. Leaders who encourage trust-building measures—like fostering dialogue between political parties and interest groups—can overcome dysfunction by focusing on shared goals.

Creating Commitment and Accountability

Commitment is essential for team alignment, but it can't exist without clarity. Teams that lack a shared vision or don't understand their individual roles often struggle to find cohesion. For leaders, the key is to communicate in a clear direction, align goals with individual contributions, and ensure that each team member knows their responsibilities.

One of the best examples of commitment-building comes from **Howard Schultz** during his tenure at Starbucks. In the face of declining sales and customer dissatisfaction in the early 2000s, Schultz realized that the company had drifted from its core mission. He took drastic steps to recommit the company to its purpose of delivering a high-quality coffee experience. Schultz even temporarily closed thousands of Starbucks locations for retraining, reinforcing the commitment to excellence among employees. This bold move reinvigorated the organization's culture, reestablishing a shared sense of purpose and accountability.

In **technological leadership accountability** becomes critical, especially when driving innovation. Leaders like **Elon Musk** Tesla and SpaceX foster a culture of high accountability by setting ambitious goals and holding teams to strict timelines and quality standards. Musk's leadership style is demanding but effective because it is built on a foundation of clear expectations and a commitment to delivering breakthrough results. He holds both himself and his team accountable for pushing boundaries while continually striving for excellence. This sense of shared responsibility fosters greater commitment to the company's mission.

Accountability also plays a pivotal role in **financial leadership,** particularly in the banking industry, where a lack of accountability has historically led to systemic dysfunction. The 2008 financial crisis was largely a result of financial institutions shirking responsibility for risky lending practices. In the years following, a shift toward greater regulatory accountability, transparency, and risk management has helped stabilize the industry. Leaders in finance, such as Christine Lagarde, former Managing Director of the International Monetary Fund, emphasizes the importance of responsibility at all levels, from individuals to institutions, to ensure sustainable financial systems.

DRIVING RESULTS THROUGH TEAM SYNERGY

Synergy is the ultimate goal of any team, where the collective output is greater than the sum of individual contributions. Achieving synergy requires collaboration, trust, and a clear sense of purpose. Leaders play a crucial role in driving this by fostering an environment where every team member feels valued and empowered to contribute their strengths.

In the realm of **social economics**Synergy can be seen in initiatives like community-based projects that leverage collective action to solve complex social problems. Consider the case of

Muhammad Yunus, founder of Grameen Bank and pioneer of microfinance. Yunus recognized that providing small loans to impoverished individuals—primarily women in rural areas—could enable them to start businesses, increase their income, and ultimately lift entire communities out of poverty. The success of microfinance is built on the principle of synergy: individuals working together, supported by small-scale financial interventions, to create large-scale social impact.

Synergy is also essential in **social security programs** like the Scandinavian welfare model, where governments, businesses, and citizens work collaboratively to achieve a high standard of living. These societies have achieved exceptional levels of social cohesion and economic prosperity by focusing on collective welfare, shared responsibilities, and mutual benefits. Leaders in these systems recognize that the strength of the whole depends on the contributions of every part, and they design policies to foster inclusivity and cooperation.

In **political leadershipSynergy** is crucial when navigating the complexities of governance. Leaders who succeed in fostering synergy often achieve significant political reforms, as seen in the leadership of **Angela Merkel** in Germany. Merkel, known for her pragmatic and inclusive approach, successfully brought together diverse political parties and interest groups to tackle challenges ranging from the Eurozone crisis to refugee resettlement. Her ability to build consensus and drive coordinated action across sectors contributed to Germany's political and economic stability during her tenure.

Overcoming team dysfunctions is one of the most significant challenges leaders face. By building trust, embracing healthy conflict, fostering commitment, and driving synergy, leaders can transform dysfunctional teams into cohesive, high-performing units. Whether in corporate settings, political leadership, social economic initiatives, or technological innovation, the principles of trust, commitment, accountability, and synergy apply across the board.

Great leaders understand that dysfunctions are natural but surmountable. They actively diagnose problems and implement solutions, just as **Howard Schultz** restructured Starbucks around a shared commitment, or **Elon Musk** drives accountability to achieve groundbreaking innovations. These leaders show us that overcoming dysfunction isn't just about fixing problems—it's about cultivating the right environment where teams can thrive and succeed, no matter the challenges they face.

Dr. Jordan Dickson

FOOD FOR THOUGHT

1. "We rise together. We fell alone. The dream comes true with team effort.

2. "Unity is strength." Great things are possible when people work together and cooperatively.

3. "Alone we can do this little; together we can do so much."

4. Every member of the team has strength of their own. Every member's strength is the team."

Chapter 6: The Science of Motivation

Motivation is one of the most studied—and most misunderstood—aspects of leadership. Traditionally, leaders have relied on the "carrot and stick" approach: reward good behavior, punish bad behavior. While this model has its place, it's far from sufficient for driving high performance in today's complex, dynamic environments. The science of motivation reveals that true, lasting motivation comes from within—it's not simply about external incentives. Instead, leaders must tap into deeper sources of motivation, focusing on autonomy, mastery, purpose, and fostering a culture of continuous growth.

Moving Beyond Carrot and Stick

The carrot-and-stick approach is a relic of the industrial age when simple, repetitive tasks dominated the workforce. In those environments, workers responded well to rewards for meeting quotas or punishments for falling short. But today's workplaces demand much more from employees. Workers are expected to think creatively, solve complex problems, and collaborate with diverse teams. For these tasks, external motivators are often ineffective or even counterproductive. In fact, research by **Daniel Pink**, author of **Drive**: The Surprising Truth About What Motivates Us, shows that external rewards can diminish performance in tasks requiring cognitive skills and creativity.

A well-known example of this comes from **Edward Deci**'s experiments in the 1970s, where participants were asked to solve puzzles. Some were paid for their efforts, while others were not. Deci found that the group paid to complete puzzles lost interest once the payments stopped, while the unpaid group continued to work on the puzzles simply for the joy of solving them. This illustrates the limits of the carrot-and-stick model: when rewards are removed, so is motivation, especially if the task requires intrinsic engagement.

Leaders need to move beyond this outdated model by understanding the underlying drivers of human behavior. Consider **Tony Hsieh,** the former CEO of Zappos, who rejected the traditional top-down management structure in favor of creating a culture of happiness. By focusing on employee satisfaction and personal fulfillment rather than external incentives, Hsieh fostered an environment where people were intrinsically motivated to do their best work, driving the company's success.

Equipping Teams with Autonomy, Mastery, and Vision

According to **Pink**The three pillars of motivation in the modern workplace are autonomy, mastery, and purpose. These elements go beyond financial incentives to tap into what truly motivates people: the desire to direct their own lives, the urge to get better at something that matters, and the need to connect to something larger than themselves.

Autonomy is perhaps the most powerful motivator, as people are naturally driven to seek control over their lives. This is evident in the rise of remote work, flexible hours, and flat organizational structures that give employees more freedom. **Elon Musk** exemplifies this with his leadership at SpaceX, where engineers are given significant autonomy to experiment, innovate, and solve problems. Musk's willingness to allow employees the space to fail—and learn from those failures—has led to breakthroughs in space exploration that many once thought impossible.

Mastery is another key motivator. People are naturally drawn to improve their skills and achieve a sense of competence in their work. Consider the case of **Google's 20% Time** policy, which allowed employees to spend 20% of their work hours on projects of their choosing. This policy wasn't just about freedom; it was about giving people the opportunity to pursue mastery. Some of Google's most successful products—such as Gmail and Google News—originated from this policy, proving that when people are given the space to cultivate their skills, innovation flourishes.

Finally, **purpose** connects employees to a higher cause. Purpose-driven companies outperform their competitors because their employees feel like they are contributing to something meaningful. A striking example is **Patagonia**, the outdoor clothing company founded by **Yvon Chouinard**. From its inception, Patagonia has operated with a deep sense of environmental responsibility, encouraging employees to engage in activism and environmental conservation efforts. This clear sense of purpose has not only motivated employees but has also created a loyal customer base that values the company's mission.

In the public sector, **social security** organizations have long struggled to motivate their employees with limited financial resources. Yet, some of the most effective social security programs—such as those in **Denmark and Sweden**—have succeeded because they focus on purpose. Employees in these systems understand that their work has a direct, positive impact on people's lives, which creates a sense of fulfillment that transcends traditional rewards.

Fostering a Culture of Continuous Growth

In a rapidly changing world, continuous growth and learning are essential for both individuals and organizations. The concept of a **growth mindset,** coined by psychologist **Carol Dweck,** emphasizes the belief that abilities can be developed through effort, learning, and persistence. Leaders who cultivate a growth mindset in their teams empower individuals to take on challenges, learn from failures, and continuously improve.

In **financial leadership** For instance, continuous growth is vital in a world of shifting markets and evolving regulations. Successful leaders in this space, such as **Warren Buffett**, prioritize lifelong learning. Buffett famously spends a significant portion of his day reading and reflecting on new information, a habit that has contributed to his sustained success in an unpredictable industry. By modeling this behavior, he encourages others to adopt a mindset of constant learning and adaptation.

In **technological leadership**, the speed of innovation demands that leaders and teams remain adaptable and forward-thinking. Consider **Microsoft's transformation under Satya Nadella**. When Nadella took over as CEO, Microsoft had fallen behind competitors in critical areas like cloud computing. To foster a culture of continuous growth, Nadella promoted a "learn-it-all" mentality, replacing the previously entrenched "know-it-all" culture. By emphasizing curiosity, experimentation, and learning from mistakes, Nadella helped revitalize Microsoft, leading the company to unprecedented growth and success.

Continuous growth also requires leaders to foster an environment where people feel safe to take risks and make mistakes. In **social economics**, initiatives like the **Grameen Bank Microfinance** programs empower entrepreneurs in developing countries to grow their businesses without the fear of failure crippling them. By providing support and resources to help individuals learn and grow, these programs enable sustainable development and long-term economic empowerment.

Understanding the science of motivation is key to unlocking the full potential of any team or organization. Moving beyond outdated carrot-and-stick models, leaders must focus on fostering autonomy, mastery, and purpose. Empowering teams in this way creates an environment where people are motivated from within, leading to higher levels of performance, innovation, and job satisfaction.

Leaders who embrace the principles of autonomy, mastery, and purpose—and who foster a culture of continuous growth—are more likely to succeed in today's complex and rapidly evolving world. Whether in technology, finance, social economics, or politics, leaders who prioritize intrinsic motivation over external rewards will find that their teams are more engaged, resilient, and innovative. The art of leadership is evolving, and the science of motivation provides the tools to build teams that thrive, regardless of the challenges they face.

DR. JORDAN DICKSON

Leadership Mastery

Part III: Strategic Tools for Success

Chapter 7: The Strategic Playbook

Imagine you're sitting across the table from a tough competitor, eyeing each other across a battlefield that isn't defined by physical boundaries but by decisions, negotiations, and calculated risks. This isn't just a game of business; it's a game of strategy. And like any game, to win, you need to understand the rules, the players, and most importantly, how to think several moves ahead. Strategic leaders, the best ones, recognize that strategy isn't static. It's a fluid, constantly evolving process that requires mastering tools such as game theory, competitive strategy, and decisive decision-making. These tools are your playbook, the foundation on which you'll build long-term success in an unpredictable world.

Applying Game Theory to Business Strategy: Thinking Like a Strategist

Game theory is often thought of as something reserved for mathematicians or economists. But the truth is, it's a framework that's deeply embedded in the most effective strategic leaders' decision-making processes. **Game theory** is essentially the science of decision-making, where you must anticipate not only your own actions but the reactions of others. Every move you make in business, every decision, every negotiation, is part of a larger game. Whether you're negotiating a deal, launching a product, or entering a new market, you're playing a game where your competitors, customers, and even partners are making moves of their own.

Take, for example, the cutthroat world of **ride-sharing services**. When **Uber** first burst onto the scene, they were the clear disruptor.

But **Lyft** quickly emerged as a rival, forcing Uber to reevaluate its strategy. Both companies were competing for dominance, and both were playing a game of strategic moves. When Uber would drop fares to attract more drivers and riders, Lyft would do the same. But Lyft recognized something critical in the game: instead of trying to match Uber's scale, they could differentiate by being the more community-oriented, "friendlier" alternative, even adding features like in-car tipping for drivers, which Uber initially resisted. This differentiation was Lyft's strategic move in the game—recognizing that they couldn't win by playing Uber's game, so they created their own.

In this way, game theory applies not only to direct competition but to the entire business landscape. Consider **Netflix** as another example. When Netflix was transitioning from a DVD rental service to a streaming giant, they anticipated not only the moves of competitors like Blockbuster but also the future behavior of consumers and technology trends. Netflix knew that competitors would eventually follow suit, but they made a key strategic move: investing heavily in original content before their competitors could catch up. Shows like **House of Cards** and **Stranger Things** became cultural phenomena, drawing millions to the platform. Netflix essentially created a new game where they were the dominant player, and by the time competitors like Amazon Prime and Hulu ramped up their original content efforts, Netflix had already built a massive lead.

Now, this idea of anticipating others' moves doesn't just apply to head-on competition. **Game theory** can also be applied to negotiations, pricing strategies, market entry, and even **internal team dynamics**. Imagine you're a tech company negotiating with a supplier. If you know that your competitor is also negotiating with the same supplier, your strategy might shift. You could lock in a long-term contract at a slightly higher price to ensure security, anticipating that your competitor might push for lower prices but shorter contracts. By understanding the supplier's incentives and the competitor's potential moves, you can navigate the negotiation more effectively, ensuring your business's long-term supply stability.

Political landscapes also provide ripe ground for game theory applications. Take global trade negotiations as an example. In 2018, the United States imposed tariffs on various goods from China, which resulted in retaliatory tariffs from China on American products. Both countries were playing a high-stakes game, each making moves to strengthen their own economic positions while anticipating the other's response. The key for leaders in such scenarios is to look beyond the immediate impact of these moves and think long-term—what will this do to supply chains? How will it impact alliances? Game theory allows leaders to play this "long game," not just reacting to the current situation but positioning themselves for future outcomes.

MASTERING COMPETITIVE STRATEGY AND EXECUTION: MOVING BEYOND THEORY

Game theory helps you understand the dynamics at play, but strategy without execution is just theory. **Michael Porter**, one of the most influential thinkers in business strategy, famously created the **Five Forces Framework**. This model emphasizes that to understand your competitive environment, you need to analyze not just your direct competitors but the entire ecosystem of your industry—suppliers, customers, potential new entrants, substitute products, and the overall intensity of competition.

Take the example of **Southwest Airlines**, a company that used Porter's principles to great effect. Southwest recognized that the traditional airline industry was stuck in a highly competitive, low-profit game. Rather than competing on the same terms—fighting over first-class passengers, offering more routes, or increasing inflight services—Southwest changed the game entirely. They focused on low-cost, no-frills flights, reducing complexity in their operations, flying only one type of plane (the Boeing 737), and avoiding the traditional hub-and-spoke model of other airlines. By doing this,

Southwest minimized operational costs and passed those savings onto their customers, ultimately creating a new competitive space where they were the uncontested leader. This is what **Porter** might be called "**creating a competitive advantage.**"

But, of course, competitive strategy is more than just cutting costs or finding a niche. It requires a deep understanding of your environment and your ability to execute effectively. A well-thought-out strategy might look brilliant on paper, but if it's not executed with precision, it can quickly fall apart. A prime example of this is **Kodak.** Despite being the pioneer of digital photography, Kodak failed to capitalize on its invention because the company couldn't let go of its film business. Their strategy was theoretically sound—digital was the future—but they failed to execute effectively due to internal resistance and fear of cannibalizing their existing revenue streams.

This is a cautionary story for leaders: even the best strategy is useless if you can't follow through with decisive action.

DECISION-MAKING IN UNCERTAIN TIMES: PLAYING THE LONG GAME

Decision-making is the heart of strategic leadership. It's where your theories, your strategies, and your plans meet reality. The most challenging decisions are often those made under uncertainty, where you don't have all the information you need, but you must act anyway. This is where leaders truly earn their stripes.

Take **Apple's decision to create the iPhone** as an example of bold decision-making. At the time, the market was dominated by Nokia and Blackberry, and the concept of a full touchscreen phone was seen as a huge gamble. But **Steve Jobs** understood that technology was shifting, and more importantly, he trusted that consumers would embrace a device that consolidated their phone, music player, and internet browser into one. This decision wasn't based on certainty—there were countless unknowns—but it was based on strategic vision and a willingness to take risks in the face of uncertainty.

Jeff Bezos has a similar approach with Amazon. When Bezos launched **Amazon Web Services (AWS)** In 2006, the idea of cloud computing was still in its infancy. Many in the tech world didn't understand why a company known for e-commerce was investing so heavily in this area. But Bezos anticipated that businesses would eventually move away from managing their own data centers to renting computing power and storage on demand. Today, AWS is one of Amazon's most profitable divisions, proving that bold, strategic decisions made in uncertain times can pay off massively.

Of course, the challenge for leaders is that they often have to make these decisions without perfect information. This is where frameworks like the **OODA Loop**—which stands for Observe, Orient, Decide, Act—come into play. Developed by military strategist **John Boyd**The OODA Loop emphasizes rapid decision-making in fast-moving environments. The key is to cycle through the loop quickly, constantly gathering new information, adapting to changes, and staying ahead of the competition.

For business leaders, applying the OODA Loop means being comfortable with ambiguity and learning to make informed decisions quickly, even when the landscape is shifting beneath you. It's about understanding that in a rapidly changing world, indecision is often the greatest risk.

The strategic playbook is more than just a collection of theories; it's a practical toolkit that leaders can use to navigate the complexities of modern business. By applying game theory, mastering competitive strategy, and making confident decisions under uncertainty, leaders can position themselves for long-term success, no matter how turbulent the environment may be. As you build your own playbook, remember that the game is always evolving, and the best leaders are those who can adapt, think several moves ahead, and execute their strategy with precision. Whether you're a seasoned executive or a rising leader, the principles of strategic leadership are universal, and they will help you win—whatever your game may be.

Chapter 8: Data-driven Leadership

In today's fast-paced, technology-driven world, leaders no longer rely solely on intuition or past experiences to guide their decisions. The era of **data-driven leadership** has dawned, where numbers, analytics, and insights are integral to crafting successful strategies. The leaders who thrive are those who know how to leverage metrics, translate data into actionable insights, and use this information to drive continuous improvement in their teams and organizations.

Leveraging Metrics and Analytics for Informed Decisions

Think about how **Google** makes decisions. Every aspect of the company's operations, from product development to customer experience, is driven by data. **Sundar Pichai**Google's CEO once noted that key product features, like the "Search" algorithm adjustments or YouTube's recommendation engine, are constantly fine-tuned through rigorous data analysis. The data gathered from billions of users isn't just about volume; it's about insight—predicting what people want, even before they know it themselves. Google's leadership is driven by the relentless pursuit of knowledge through data.

But how do you, as a leader, leverage metrics and analytics to inform decisions? It starts with identifying the **key performance indicators (KPIs)** that are most relevant to your organization's success. Whether it's customer retention rates, employee productivity, or sales growth, understanding these critical metrics allows you to see not just where you stand, but also to predict where you're headed.

Take **Tesla** for instance. **Elon Musk** doesn't just rely on his visionary instincts; he also pays close attention to data. Tesla's autopilot system is continuously improved based on vast amounts of real-time data collected from every Tesla car on the road. Each mile driven contributes to the improvement of their AI, making the system safer and more efficient over time. This is data-driven leadership in action—every decision, from minor software updates to major product innovations, is grounded in data analytics.

Turning Insights into Action

Having access to data is one thing; knowing how to act on it is what separates great leaders from the rest. Many organizations collect mountains of data but fail to harness its power effectively. For data-driven leadership to truly work, leaders must be able to translate insights into concrete actions.

Consider how **Howard Schultz** transformed **Starbucks**. During his second stint as CEO, Schultz faced a declining market and weakening customer loyalty. Instead of reacting emotionally or impulsively, he turned to data. He studied customer behaviors, preferences, and feedback, which revealed that the Starbucks experience was losing its appeal due to rapid expansion and operational inefficiencies. Schultz acted on these insights by closing underperforming stores, revamping the in-store experience, and retraining employees. As a result, Starbucks rebounded, reinforcing the power of using data to make informed and impactful decisions.

Turning insights into action involves a structured approach. It requires breaking down the data into manageable pieces, understanding the story it tells, and then translating it into actionable steps. For example, socio **economic leaders** might gather data on economic trends and consumer spending patterns. By analyzing this data, they can determine where to invest, how to price products, or when to launch new initiatives that align with market demand. This application of data can help identify opportunities for growth or reveal inefficiencies that need to be addressed.

In the **political landscape** data-driven leadership can be seen in the campaign strategies of successful politicians. **Barack Obama's 2008 presidential campaign** was a watershed moment for data in politics. His team used voter data, social media analytics, and advanced algorithms to micro-target voters, optimize advertising efforts, and shape campaign messaging in real-time. The ability to turn voter data into targeted actions allowed Obama to engage with previously untapped voter segments, which ultimately helped secure his victory.

Tracking Progress for Continuous Improvement

Data-driven leadership is not a one-time initiative. It's an ongoing process of tracking, measuring, and adjusting based on the insights gained. Continuous improvement is the ultimate goal. Leaders who use data effectively are always asking, "How can we do better?"

In the **financial sector**, this approach can be observed through **investment firms** that leverage data to optimize their portfolios. By consistently monitoring the performance of their investments, they can make quick decisions to rebalance portfolios in response to market shifts. Firms like **BlackRock** use advanced algorithms and data analytics to track everything from stock performance to global economic indicators. This constant tracking allows them to make informed decisions, ensuring they maximize returns for their clients while minimizing risks.

On a smaller scale, businesses like **Zappos** have embraced the concept of continuous improvement by fostering a culture of data-driven decision-making at all levels. Zappos tracks customer satisfaction metrics religiously and uses this data to refine their customer service approach. By keeping an eye on trends and staying flexible in their strategy, they maintain one of the highest customer satisfaction rates in the e-commerce industry.

In **technological fields**Data tracking can also lead to product improvements. Think about **Apple's approach** to product design and customer experience. Apple continually collects data from its devices, analyzing how customers use their products. When the Apple Watch was first introduced, it lacked many health and fitness features that are now standard. Over time, Apple gathered data on how users interacted with the Watch, which led them to develop features like heart rate monitoring and ECG capabilities, turning the device into a personal health companion. Apple's use of data to improve product design exemplifies how tracking progress can drive continuous improvement.

Empowering Data-Driven Leadership

Data-driven leadership is about empowering yourself and your team with the information necessary to make smarter, faster, and more impactful decisions. Leaders who embrace metrics, translate insights into actions, and continuously track their progress can position themselves at the forefront of their industries. Whether you're navigating the world of business, politics, social economics, or technology, the data is there to guide you—if you're willing to listen and act. The most successful leaders of the modern era aren't just those with bold visions; they are the ones who know how to turn data into a strategic asset. By adopting data-driven leadership, you not only improve decision-making but also foster a culture of growth, accountability, and adaptability, ensuring that your organization stays ahead in an ever-changing world.

Chapter 9: Creating Uncontested Markets

In the world of business strategy, few ideas have reshaped leadership thinking as much as the concept of **Blue Ocean Strategy**. Coined by **W. Chan Kim and Renée Mauborgne**, it introduced a powerful approach to creating uncontested markets where competition becomes irrelevant. It's a way of breaking away from the conventional cutthroat race that most businesses engage in and discovering entirely new frontiers where opportunities abound.

Let's start by imagining two distinct environments—red oceans and blue oceans. Red oceans are where traditional competition takes place. Think of industries like fast food, airlines, or traditional retail. In these spaces, everyone is fighting for the same customers, and as a result, profits thin out, prices drop, and businesses engage in fierce battles for survival. Now contrast this with blue oceans—new market spaces that are ripe for innovation, where businesses can chart new courses and escape the competition altogether. It's like entering uncharted waters where you are the only ship.

Identifying Blue Oceans and Opportunities

Finding a blue ocean isn't about chasing the latest trend or innovating for innovation's sake. It's about carefully identifying opportunities where unmet needs exist and creating value in ways that your competitors aren't even thinking about. **Apple** provides a textbook example of blue ocean creation. Before the launch of the iPhone, the smartphone market was highly fragmented and dominated by companies focused primarily on tech specifications and business users. Apple, instead of competing within this red ocean, created a blue ocean by reimagining what a smartphone could be—focusing on design, ease of use, and creating an ecosystem that integrated seamlessly across their products. The iPhone, iPad, and Mac all worked together, locking users into the Apple ecosystem, which was not only innovative but also immensely profitable.

Another example is **Cirque du Soleil**. When it launched in the 1980s, the circus industry was struggling. Audiences were dwindling, competition was intense, and traditional circuses were losing their appeal. Rather than compete with existing circuses, Cirque du Soleil created a new kind of experience by blending acrobatics with artistic storytelling, eliminating costly elements like animal acts, and charging premium prices for a sophisticated show. They didn't compete; they reinvented the circus, creating a blue ocean of opportunity.

For leaders, identifying blue oceans requires a mindset that prioritizes **looking beyond existing demand** and discovering the latent potential within markets. It's not always about creating a completely new product but about rethinking how you deliver value. Take **Netflix** as another example. When it transitioned from DVD rentals to streaming, Netflix didn't just find a blue ocean; it created one. By anticipating shifts in consumer behavior and leveraging emerging technology, Netflix effectively created a new market where it had a significant first-mover advantage. Today, it continues to dominate, thanks to that initial leap into an uncontested space.

DIFFERENTIATING THROUGH INNOVATION

Innovation is the engine that drives successful blue ocean strategies. But the key to innovation isn't just developing new products; it's about redefining customer experiences and solving problems in ways others haven't considered.

Think about **Tesla**. While the automobile industry is notoriously competitive, Tesla didn't simply launch another electric vehicle. Instead, **Elon Musk** created a luxury electric car brand that also happened to be high-performance, tech-savvy, and sustainable.

Tesla's differentiation strategy wasn't just about the cars themselves; it was about revolutionizing the entire driving and ownership experience. By providing over-the-air software updates, an ever-growing Supercharger network, and self-driving capabilities, Tesla set itself apart from traditional automakers that were bogged down in incremental changes.

Another great example of differentiation through innovation is **Amazon**. **Jeff Bezos** didn't just build an online store; he created a platform that constantly innovated in logistics, technology, and customer service. Amazon's use of **AI-driven recommendations**, their **Prime membership model**, and their ability to deliver products within hours sets them apart. Bezos' relentless focus on the customer ensured that Amazon didn't just compete in the retail space—they owned it by differentiating their entire value proposition.

In social and political contexts, innovation can also create blue oceans. For example, **Muhammad Yunus,** the founder of **Grameen Bank,** created a new financial market by pioneering microcredit loans for the poor. Traditional banks wouldn't lend to people with no collateral, but Yunus found a blue ocean in serving an underserved population with small, sustainable loans, transforming lives and economies in the process.

For leaders, differentiating through innovation means continually asking, "What's the customer problem we can solve better?" or "**How can we change the game?**" The focus should always be on creating new value—not just for the business, but for the customer.

SCALING SUSTAINABLE SUCCESS

Making a blue ocean marks only one phase of the journey. The next challenge is to scale that success sustainably. Many businesses find a blue ocean but struggle to maintain momentum as the market shifts or competitors begin to take notice. Scaling your innovation while protecting your unique value is key to staying ahead.

Uber, for instance, revolutionized the transportation industry by creating a blue ocean in the ride-sharing market. But scaling this success came with challenges. As Uber expanded, it faced regulatory hurdles, competition from other ride-sharing companies like Lyft, and internal issues like driver dissatisfaction. To sustain its growth, Uber had to continually innovate, expanding into food delivery, freight, and even autonomous vehicles. The lesson here is that scaling sustainably means anticipating new challenges, evolving your offering, and staying ahead of the curve.

Howard Schultz, in scaling **Starbucks**, ensured the brand's growth was sustainable by investing heavily in the company's culture and maintaining a focus on the core values that made Starbucks a success in the first place. As the company grew, Schultz focused on preserving the customer experience, whether by introducing new products like cold brew and nitro coffee, redesigning stores to feel more inviting, or maintaining high standards for customer service. Scaling sustainably meant that Starbucks could grow without losing sight of its original vision.

Sustainability also plays a role in the long-term success of businesses within social, economic, and environmental landscapes. Patagonia, for example, has scaled its success not by focusing solely on profit but by staying true to its commitment to sustainability and ethical practices. By ensuring that their products are environmentally friendly and supporting grassroots environmental initiatives, Patagonia has not only scaled sustainably but has built a loyal customer base that values its ethical stance.

In creating uncontested markets, leaders need to think beyond initial success. Sustainable scaling involves creating systems and processes that allow the business to grow without compromising its values, quality, or customer relationships. This requires strategic planning, continual innovation, and a dedication to staying ahead of market shifts.

The pursuit of blue oceans is about creating new frontiers of opportunity—where your business can flourish, innovate, and scale in ways that traditional competition cannot. By identifying underserved markets, differentiating through meaningful innovation, and scaling sustainably, leaders have the chance to carve out a space where they can thrive, setting themselves apart from the pack. In today's world, where change is constant, leaders who can create uncontested markets will not only survive but will define the future.

DR. JORDAN DICKSON
Leadership Mastery

Part IV: Personal Development and Resilience

Chapter 10: The Beauty of Imperfection

In leadership, we often think of strength in terms of confidence, authority, and control. However, one of the most powerful gifts a leader can possess is the ability to embrace imperfection and vulnerability. This idea is at the core of Brené Brown's work, particularly in her book The Gifts of Imperfection. Brown emphasizes that embracing our vulnerabilities is not a weakness but rather a courageous act that fosters personal growth, connection, and resilience.

Embracing Vulnerability for Personal Growth

Vulnerability often carries a stigma of weakness, especially in leadership roles. Leaders are expected to have all the answers, to always be in control, and to never falter. However, the reality is that no leader is perfect, and the willingness to embrace that imperfection can be a key driver of growth. When you are open about your struggles and uncertainties, you not only create space for self-improvement but also set an example for others.

Take the story of **Howard Schultz**, the former CEO of Starbucks. When Schultz came back to Starbucks in 2008, the firm was floundering. Sales were declining, and Starbucks had lost its way. Rather than pretending everything was fine, Schultz openly admitted his mistakes and took responsibility for the company's decline. He called a company-wide meeting, closed hundreds of stores for a day, and retrained employees on the art of making espresso. By embracing his vulnerability, Schultz created a culture of transparency and accountability within Starbucks, ultimately leading the company back to success.

Personal growth as a leader begins with the willingness to accept that you don't know everything. Leaders who embrace vulnerability are better able to reflect on their experiences, learn from their mistakes, and foster an environment where continuous learning is valued.

OVERCOMING FEAR AND SHAME IN LEADERSHIP

Leadership often comes with fear—fear of failure, fear of not being enough, fear of being judged. These fears can manifest as shame, which can be paralyzing. However, facing these fears head-on is a crucial step in developing resilience. **Brené Brown** discusses how shame can undermine our ability to lead effectively, but by recognizing and working through it, we can become stronger.

Consider **Michael Jordan**, often regarded as the greatest basketball player of all time. Despite his legendary status, Jordan was cut from his high school basketball team. That rejection could have easily filled him with shame, but instead of letting it define him, Jordan used it as fuel to push harder. He famously stated, "I've failed over and over and over again in my life. And that is why I succeed." Overcoming the fear of failure and shame allowed Jordan to rise to incredible heights, and that same mindset is critical for leaders. When leaders address their fears openly, they empower themselves and their teams to take risks without the burden of shame. This creates a culture where failure is seen as a stepping stone to success, rather than something to be feared or hidden.

NURTURING COURAGE, COMPASSION, AND CONNECTION

At the heart of leadership is **courage**—the courage to be vulnerable, to take risks, to face the unknown. But courage alone isn't enough. Effective leadership also requires **compassion** and the ability to create meaningful **connections** with others.

Compassion in leadership means understanding that everyone, including yourself, is a work in progress. Leaders who practice compassion are more attuned to the needs of their team members and more willing to offer support when it's needed. Compassion also fosters trust, which is essential for creating strong connections within a team.

A powerful example of compassionate leadership is the story of **Arne Sorenson,** the late CEO of Marriott International. Sorenson led the company through the early days of the COVID-19 pandemic, a time of great uncertainty for the hospitality industry. In an emotional video message to employees, Sorenson acknowledged the pain and fear they were experiencing and made difficult decisions to ensure the company's survival while showing deep empathy for the impact those decisions had on Marriott's people. Sorenson's vulnerability and compassion during that challenging time helped foster a sense of solidarity and connection within the organization, even in the face of unprecedented adversity.

Leaders who embrace imperfection understand that they don't need to have all the answers. Instead, they rely on their team, cultivate strong connections through empathy and compassion, and foster an environment where everyone is encouraged to grow. Courage, compassion, and connection are the cornerstones of this leadership philosophy, and they create a foundation of trust that allows teams to thrive, even in challenging times.

The gifts of imperfection—vulnerability, courage, compassion, and connection—are what make a leader truly great. By embracing imperfection, leaders can unlock personal growth, overcome fear and shame, and build stronger, more resilient teams. In a world that often values perfectionism, it's the leaders who are willing to admit their flaws and grow from them that inspire the most loyalty and respect. The greatest leaders are not those who avoid failure, but those who have the courage to face it, learn from it, and rise above it with compassion and strength.

1. "Embracing our imperfections is the key to living a wholehearted, authentic life."

2. "Imperfections are affirmations that we all are in this together; they are not limitations."

3. "The beauty of imperfection is that it's an inherent aspect of life."

4. "By embracing our imperfections, we open ourselves up to connection, creativity, and joy."

"Imperfections are the threads that weave our unique stories, making us stronger, more resilient, and wonderfully imperfect."

Chapter 11: The Leader's Growth Mindset

Growth is a powerful force, but in leadership, it isn't something that happens by accident or coincidence. It is the result of a dedicated mindset—one that thrives on continuous learning, reflection, and the ability to adapt through adversity. Leadership, after all, isn't about achieving a particular position or status; it's about the never-ending journey of becoming better, more resilient, and more insightful over time.

Let me share a story about a CEO named Michael, who found himself at the helm of a struggling manufacturing company. The market was evolving, and his company was being left behind. Michael had two options: stay stuck in old ways or embrace change. But what was holding him back was not a lack of ideas—it was his mindset. He had spent years building this business with a specific way of thinking, and now the world had shifted around him. His fear of stepping into unfamiliar territory weighed on him. But after deep reflection, he recognized that growth would only come from unlearning outdated habits and relearning what it means to lead in this new environment.

This moment of realization is what marks a **growth mindset**. Michael immersed himself in learning new strategies, engaged with younger, more dynamic teams, and sought mentorship from leaders outside his industry. Through that mindset shift, he was able to pivot his company's strategy, and within two years, they were back on track, thriving in new markets. What Michael discovered wasn't just a business strategy—it was the personal transformation that fueled his ability to lead through ambiguity and change.

Growth-minded leaders understand that their development is just as critical as the growth of the company they lead. **Bill Gates** exemplifies this. Despite leading one of the most successful technology companies in the world, Gates has always prioritized self-education. He devours books across subjects like history, technology, and business—not because he has to, but because he knows that continuous learning is essential to staying relevant in an ever-evolving world. His transformation from Microsoft's co-founder to a global philanthropist happened because of this relentless dedication to personal growth.

Lifelong Learning

Learning is more than just acquiring information; it's about having the humility to recognize that you don't know everything and the curiosity to constantly seek out new knowledge. It's about staying open to fresh ideas, no matter your age, experience, or accomplishments. In practice, this looks like making time in your busy schedule to read, listen, and engage with others who might have perspectives different from your own. It's in the openness to ask questions, to mentor and be mentored, and to explore unfamiliar terrain, intellectually and emotionally.

But what really takes this kind of leadership to the next level is **self-reflection**. Think of **Ray Dalio,** the billionaire founder of Bridgewater Associates, who is widely known for his practice of logging his mistakes and reflecting on them systematically. He believes in radical transparency and uses his reflections to continuously adjust and grow—not only as a leader but also as a person. When Dalio makes a decision, he looks back on it, analyzes what went right or wrong, and uses that knowledge to make better decisions in the future. This level of introspection is what separates truly great leaders from the rest. Self-reflection doesn't mean wallowing in past mistakes; it's about extracting lessons from those experiences, using them to sharpen your perspective, and making better choices moving forward.

RESILIENCE AND SELF-CARE

Resilience, too, is a core component of the growth mindset. Resilience isn't simply about enduring difficult times—it's about thriving in them. It's about finding strength not only to survive adversity but to come out stronger on the other side. When you lead with resilience, you're constantly recalibrating, bouncing back, and learning from whatever challenges are thrown your way.

Let's look at **Howard Schultz**, the former CEO of Starbucks. His resilience was tested when he returned to the company in 2008 during a financial crisis. Starbucks had overextended itself, quality had dropped, and the brand was losing its luster. Schultz didn't shy away from the difficult reality. Instead, he made tough decisions—closing hundreds of stores, retraining staff, and refocusing on the company's core values. He remained resilient in the face of massive pressure and criticism. Schultz's resilience, paired with a growth mindset, allowed Starbucks to regain its strength and reestablish itself as a global powerhouse.

When you cultivate resilience, you begin to see setbacks not as dead ends but as turning points. Resilient leaders understand that it's not just about how they weather the storm, but how they emerge from it—stronger, wiser, and more focused. Resilience in leadership requires accepting that failure is part of the process and understanding that the path to success is paved with moments of learning and adaptation.

But none of this growth—whether through learning, reflection, or resilience—can be sustained without **self-care**. Leadership is an intensely demanding role, both mentally and physically. Leaders are often driven, passionate, and highly focused on their goals. But as Arianna Huffington discovered, driving yourself to the brink of burnout is counterproductive. When Huffington collapsed from exhaustion, it was a wake-up call. She realized that leading a successful life required not just achieving more but also taking care of her mind, body, and spirit.

For leaders, self-care isn't a luxury—it's a necessity. It means ensuring that you are functioning at your best, whether that involves taking breaks, prioritizing sleep, engaging in hobbies, or spending time with loved ones. It also means paying attention to your mental health, which is just as important as your physical well-being. A leader who is burned out and exhausted cannot lead effectively; therefore, incorporating renewal practices into your routine is essential for sustaining high levels of performance over the long haul.

This idea of self-care extends into all aspects of leadership. It's about creating a healthy work-life balance, recognizing the importance of rest and reflection, and giving yourself the permission to recharge. Leaders who practice self-care are more creative, more focused, and better equipped to handle the stresses of leadership. They understand that to lead others effectively, they must first take care of themselves.

The growth mindset, therefore, is not just about accumulating knowledge or achieving business success. It's a holistic approach to leadership that involves cultivating personal resilience, nurturing your own well-being, and continuously learning and reflecting. It's the mindset that sees challenges as opportunities, failures as lessons, and success as an ongoing journey of development. Leaders who adopt this mindset are not just better equipped to handle the complexities of the modern world—they are also more fulfilled, more adaptable, and more capable of leading with authenticity and vision.

In every stage of leadership, whether you're a seasoned executive or just starting out, the growth mindset is the compass that guides you toward becoming a better leader and a better version of yourself. Embrace it, nurture it, and let it be the foundation upon which you build not just your career, but your legacy.

Chapter 12: Finding Meaning In Leadership

Leadership isn't just about achieving targets or driving profits—it's about something much more profound. At its heart, true leadership is about finding and living with purpose. It's about connecting the work we do every day to something bigger than ourselves, something that resonates deeply with our values and aspirations. This sense of purpose is what transforms ordinary leaders into extraordinary ones, creating a legacy that endures long after they're gone.

Leading with Purpose Beyond Profit

When we think about leadership, especially in a business context, profit is often the first thing that comes to mind. But the most impactful leaders are those who lead with a purpose that transcends the bottom line. These are the leaders who understand that while profit is essential for survival, it's purpose that drives true success and fulfillment.

Take **Howard Schultz**, the former CEO of Starbucks, as an example. Schultz didn't just want to sell coffee; he wanted to create a sense of community—a "third place" between work and home where people could connect. His vision was about much more than coffee; it was about human connection, treating employees with respect, and creating a company culture that prioritized people over profits. This purpose-driven approach was not only morally sound but also made Starbucks a global powerhouse. Under Schultz's leadership, Starbucks became synonymous with more than just a cup of coffee; it became a place where people felt valued and connected, fostering a loyal customer base that drove the company's success.

Similarly, **Blake Mycoskie,** the founder of TOMS Shoes, built his company on a simple yet powerful principle: for every pair of shoes sold, a pair would be given to a child in need. This one-for-one model wasn't just a marketing gimmick; it was the heart of the business. Mycoskie's purpose was to make a difference in the world, and he built a business that did just that. TOMS has since expanded its giving model to include eyewear, clean water, and safe birth initiatives. By leading with a purpose beyond profit, Mycoskie created a company that not only thrived commercially but also left a positive impact on millions of lives worldwide.

Nelson Mandela offers a powerful example of purpose-driven leadership in the political arena. Mandela's life was marked by his unwavering commitment to justice, equality, and reconciliation. After spending 27 years in prison, he emerged not with a desire for revenge but with a vision for a united South Africa. Mandela's leadership was rooted in a deep purpose: to dismantle apartheid and build a nation where all people could live together in peace and equality. His purpose-driven approach helped to heal a divided country and established him as a global symbol of hope, justice, and moral leadership. Mandela's legacy is a testament to the profound impact that purpose can have, not just on a leader's immediate sphere of influence, but on the world at large.

In the business world, **Elon Musk** exemplifies leading with purpose beyond profit. Musk's ventures, from Tesla to SpaceX, are driven by his mission to secure humanity's future. With Tesla, Musk is not just making electric cars; he's pushing the boundaries of sustainability, aiming to reduce the world's dependence on fossil fuels and combat climate change. SpaceX, on the other hand, is not just about space exploration; it's about making life multi-planetary, ensuring the long-term survival of humanity. Musk's purpose-driven leadership attracts not only consumers but also top talent who are motivated by the chance to work on projects that matter for the future of our planet and species.

Purpose-driven leadership isn't confined to the business or political realms. In the world of **social entrepreneurship,** purpose often takes precedence over profit. Leaders in this space are motivated by a desire to solve social problems and create positive change. Their work serves as a reminder that leadership, at its best, is about more than personal or organizational gain; it's about making a meaningful impact on the world.

SEEKING ANSWERS TO LIFE'S BIG QUESTIONS

To truly understand the importance of finding meaning in leadership, we can turn to the profound insights of Viktor E. Frankl in his seminal work, **Man's Search for Meaning**. Frankl, a psychiatrist and Holocaust survivor, argues that the primary drive in human beings is not pleasure, as Freud suggested, but the pursuit of meaning. Frankl's experiences in Nazi concentration camps led him to realize that even in the most horrific circumstances, people who found meaning in their suffering were more likely to survive. This search for meaning, he argues, is the cornerstone of a fulfilling life.

Frankl's insights are incredibly relevant to leadership. Leaders who find meaning in their work are more resilient, more motivated, and more effective. They are able to navigate challenges and setbacks with a sense of purpose that drives them forward, even in the face of adversity. This sense of meaning not only sustains leaders but also inspires those around them, creating a ripple effect that can transform organizations and communities.

One of the key lessons from Frankl's work is the importance of purpose in sustaining motivation and drive. When leaders connect their work to a higher purpose, they are more likely to persevere through difficulties and remain committed to their goals. This is because they see their work as part of something larger than themselves—something that has real significance and value. This sense of purpose is what keeps leaders going, even when the road gets tough.

In the context of leadership, finding meaning is not just about personal fulfillment; it's about creating a sense of shared purpose that unites and motivates others. Leaders who articulate a clear and compelling purpose can inspire their teams to work towards a common goal, fostering a sense of belonging and commitment. This shared sense of purpose is what drives organizations to achieve great things, even in the face of significant challenges.

THE LEGACY OF A LEADER: IMPACT AND SIGNIFICANCE

Ultimately, the true measure of leadership is not in the profits earned or the accolades received, but in the legacy left behind. The legacy of a leader is defined by the impact they have on the lives of others and the world around them. Leaders who find meaning in their work leave behind more than just successful organizations; they leave behind a lasting imprint on the hearts and minds of those they lead.

One of the most enduring examples of a leader's legacy is that of **Nelson Mandela**. Mandela's legacy is not measured in economic terms but in the profound social and political changes he brought about. His leadership helped to dismantle apartheid, heal a divided nation, and set South Africa on a path towards democracy and equality. Mandela's legacy is a testament to the power of purpose-driven leadership and the lasting impact it can have on the world.

In the business world, the legacy of a leader is often seen in the culture and values they instill within their organizations. **Howard Schultz** left a legacy at Starbucks that goes far beyond coffee. His commitment to creating a company that values people—both customers and employees—has had a lasting impact on the company's culture and success. Even after Schultz stepped down as CEO, the values he championed continue to shape the way Starbucks operates, influencing everything from employee benefits to customer service.

The legacy of **Blake Mycoskie** and TOMS Shoes is another powerful example. Mycoskie's one-for-one model has inspired countless other businesses to adopt similar social impact initiatives, creating a ripple effect of positive change. His leadership has shown that it is possible to build a successful business while also making a significant impact on the world. The legacy of TOMS is not just in the shoes sold or the profits earned, but in the millions of lives that have been touched by the company's giving programs.

In the realm of **technological innovation, Elon Musk** is building a legacy that could shape the future of humanity. Musk's work with Tesla and SpaceX is not just about building companies; it's about addressing some of the biggest challenges facing our planet and our species. Whether it's reducing our reliance on fossil fuels or ensuring the long-term survival of humanity, Musk's leadership is driven by a sense of purpose that goes far beyond profit. His legacy will likely be defined not just by the companies he built, but by the future he helped to create.

Leadership with purpose leaves a lasting legacy, not only in the organizations and communities we lead but in the world at large. As leaders, we must continually ask ourselves: What do we stand for? What is the legacy we wish to leave behind? Purpose is the compass that guides us toward meaningful and impactful leadership. By leading with purpose, we create not just successful organizations, but lasting, positive change in the world.

As you reflect on your own leadership journey, consider the impact you want to have—the legacy you want to leave behind. Leadership is not just about achieving goals or driving results; it's about finding meaning in the work you do and inspiring others to do the same. By leading with purpose, you can create a legacy that endures, making a difference not just in your organization, but in the lives of the people you lead and the world you serve.

Chapter 13: Practical Management for Leadership Mastery

Balancing Empathy, Execution, and Growth

Leadership is often viewed through the lens of strategy, innovation, and vision. While these elements are undeniably crucial, there's an often-overlooked facet that can make or break a leader's effectiveness: the ability to balance empathy, execution, and growth. Strategic leadership isn't just about charting the course for an organization—it's about understanding the people who will travel that course with you, ensuring that every action is aligned with a clear purpose, and fostering an environment where growth is not just possible but inevitable.

Empathy as a Strategic Tool

Empathy in leadership might sound like a soft skill, but in reality, it's one of the most powerful tools a strategic leader can wield. To lead effectively, you must first understand the people you are leading—their motivations, fears, strengths, and weaknesses. Empathy allows you to connect with your team on a deeper level, which is essential for building trust and loyalty.

Consider Howard Schultz, Starbucks' former chief executive officer. Schultz grew up in a poor family, watching his father struggle with low-paying jobs that offered no benefits. This personal experience shaped his approach to leadership. When he took the helm at Starbucks, he was determined to create a different kind of company—one that treated its employees, whom he referred to as "partners," with respect and care. Schultz introduced healthcare benefits for part-time workers, a move that was revolutionary at the time. This decision wasn't just an act of kindness; it was a strategic move that built a loyal, dedicated workforce. Schultz understood that by taking care of his employees, they would, in turn, take care of the customers, leading to a thriving business.

But empathy in leadership goes beyond policies and benefits. It's about building a society in which individuals find worth and resonance. Consider a manager in a tech startup, overseeing a team working on a groundbreaking project. The pressure to deliver is immense, and the stakes are high. Without empathy, the manager might push the team relentlessly, leading to burnout and disengagement. However, an empathetic leader would recognize the signs of stress, offer support, and create an environment where team members feel comfortable sharing their concerns. This approach not only helps to maintain the team's well-being but also ensures that they are motivated and focused on achieving their goals.

Empathy, therefore, is not just about being kind—it's a strategic advantage. By understanding and addressing the needs of your team, you create a foundation of trust and loyalty, which are essential for driving long-term success.

The Power of Clear Communication

Strategic leadership is mostly based on good communication. It's not enough to have a brilliant vision; you must be able to articulate that vision in a way that inspires and motivates others. This is where many leaders falter. They have grand ideas but struggle to convey them in a manner that resonates with their audience.

Elon Musk, the CEO of Tesla and SpaceX, is a master of clear communication. Musk is known for his ability to distill complex, technical concepts into simple, compelling messages that anyone can understand. When he talks about his vision for SpaceX, he doesn't get bogged down in the intricacies of rocket science. Instead, he talks about the future of humanity—about making life multiplanetary and securing our species' future. This kind of messaging captures the imagination and inspires people to get behind his mission.

In your own leadership journey, think about how you communicate your vision. Are you using language that is clear and accessible, or are you unintentionally alienating your audience with jargon and complexity? Remember, your team needs to understand not just what you're doing, but why you're doing it. Clear communication ensures that everyone is aligned with the mission and moving in the same direction.

However, communication is not just about clarity; it's also about consistency. A leader who frequently changes their message or strategy creates confusion and erodes trust. Consider a financial services company undergoing a major transformation. The CEO announces a new strategy to pivot towards digital services, but within a few months, the focus shifts back to traditional offerings. This back-and-forth leaves employees unsure of the company's direction, leading to disengagement and a lack of commitment to the new initiatives. In contrast, a leader who communicates a consistent message builds confidence and ensures that the entire organization is aligned with the strategic vision.

EXECUTION: TURNING VISION INTO REALITY

Having a clear vision and communicating it effectively is only part of the equation. The real challenge lies in execution—turning that vision into reality. This is where many leaders stumble. They are great at crafting a strategy but struggle to implement it effectively.

Take **Michael**, a manager who was known for his **empathetic leadership style.** His team loved working with him because he always took the time to listen to their concerns and support them. However, Michael's team often missed deadlines and struggled to meet their targets. The problem wasn't a lack of effort; it was a lack of clear direction. Michael realized that while he was good at building relationships, he needed to improve his execution skills.

To address this, Michael started setting specific, measurable goals for his team. He introduced regular check-ins to monitor progress and provided constructive feedback to keep everyone on track. By combining his empathetic leadership style with a more structured approach to execution, Michael was able to significantly improve his team's performance. They not only met their targets but also exceeded them, thanks to the clear direction and accountability he provided.

Execution also requires flexibility. Your best plans will always fall short in some way. A strategic leader must be able to adapt to changing circumstances and adjust their plans accordingly. Consider a scenario where a tech company launches a new product that initially performs well in the market. However, a competitor quickly releases a similar product with more advanced features, threatening the company's market share. A leader who rigidly sticks to the original plan might fail to respond to this threat, leading to a decline in sales. In contrast, a flexible leader would recognize the need to pivot, perhaps by accelerating the development of new features or exploring new markets. This ability to adapt ensures that the company remains competitive and continues to grow.

Fostering Growth and Development

One of the most rewarding aspects of leadership is the opportunity to foster growth within your team. A strategic leader doesn't just focus on the short-term results; they invest in the long-term development of their people. This means creating an environment where individuals are encouraged to learn, take on new challenges, and continuously improve.

Let's look at an example from the world of social economics. Imagine a leader working in a non-profit organization focused on improving education in underserved communities. The team is passionate about their mission, but they often feel overwhelmed by the challenges they face. The leader recognizes that in order to sustain their efforts, the team needs to develop new skills and approaches. They arrange for training sessions on grant writing, community engagement, and innovative teaching methods. They also encourage team members to attend conferences and networking events to broaden their perspectives.

By investing in their team's growth, the leader not only enhances their capacity to achieve the organization's mission but also fosters a culture of continuous learning. Team members feel valued and supported, which boosts their motivation and commitment to the cause.

This approach is equally important in the corporate world. Consider a leader in a financial services firm who wants to encourage innovation. Instead of micromanaging every project, they create opportunities for team members to experiment with new ideas and take calculated risks. They provide the resources and support needed to explore these ideas, but they also hold team members accountable for their results. This balance of autonomy and accountability creates a fertile ground for innovation, leading to breakthroughs that drive the company's growth.

LEAVING A LASTING LEGACY

The ultimate goal of strategic leadership is to create a lasting impact—a legacy that endures long after you've moved on. This legacy is not just about the success of the leader but the enduring success of the team and organization they leave behind.

Steve Jobs is perhaps one of the most famous examples of a leader who left a lasting legacy. Jobs didn't just build products; he built a company culture that values creativity, excellence, and continuous improvement. Even after his passing, Apple has continued to lead the industry, thanks to the systems and culture Jobs put in place. His legacy is not just the products but the sustainable success of the company.

But you don't have to be Steve Jobs to leave a legacy. Every leader, in their own way, has the opportunity to create a lasting impact. This could be through the systems you build, the people you mentor, or the values you instill in your organization. A manager in a small business who takes the time to mentor their team and build a strong company culture is leaving a legacy that will endure long after they've moved on.

In the context of a social security organization, a leader who implements innovative processes that improve efficiency and customer service is creating a legacy that benefits both the employees and the people they serve. Their impact extends beyond the immediate results, contributing to the long-term success and reputation of the organization.

As we've explored in this chapter, strategic leadership is a delicate balance of empathy, execution, and growth. A truly effective leader understands that these elements are not mutually exclusive—they are interconnected and must be integrated into every aspect of leadership.

Empathy allows you to connect with your team and understand their needs, building the trust and loyalty necessary for long-term success. Clear communication ensures that your vision is understood and embraced by everyone in the organization. Effective execution turns that vision into reality, driving the results that propel your organization forward. And by fostering a culture of growth and development, you ensure that your team is continually improving, adapting, and innovating.

Ultimately, the legacy of a strategic leader is measured not just by the success they achieve during their tenure but by the enduring impact they leave behind. By balancing empathy, execution, and growth, you can create a legacy that transcends individual achievements and contributes to the lasting success of your organization and the people you lead.

DR. JORDAN DICKSON

Leadership Mastery

Part V: Achieving Greatness

FOOD FOR THOUGHT

1. "Excellence is a choice, not a circumstance."

2. "Leadership is about modesty and relentless commitment."

3. "Clarity of purpose is the foundation of greatness."

4. "Discipline is the bridge between goals and greatness."

5. "Sustained success requires a relentless pursuit of excellence."

6. "Greatness is achieved by those who focus on the essentials and ignore the noise."

7. "Leaders that give humility and honesty first priority foster an outstanding culture based on confidence."

8. "The path to greatness is paved with difficult decisions and disciplined action."

Chapter 14: From Good to Great: The Path to Sustained Success

Achieving greatness is not a momentary accomplishment but a journey—a continuous path that requires discipline, strategy, and relentless commitment to excellence. Leadership, when executed effectively, transforms organizations from good to great, creating a culture of success that persists over time. Greatness is not just about initial success, but about sustaining it, overcoming challenges, and driving consistent growth.

This chapter draws from the core principles in **Jim Collins' Good to Great**, but also builds on them with practical illustrations and scenarios that are essential for navigating the complexities of modern leadership.

Developing Level 5 Leadership

Great organizations are driven by great leaders, but not the type of leader that many people might expect. The best leaders aren't the loudest or most charismatic. They are often quiet, humble, and fiercely determined. Collins defines this type of leader as a Level 5 Leader—someone who possesses a rare blend of personal humility and professional will. These leaders channel their ambition into the success of the organization, rather than into their own personal glory.

Consider the example of **Darwin Smith,** former CEO of Kimberly-Clark, who exemplified Level 5 Leadership. When Smith took over, the company was struggling. Against the advice of many, he made the bold decision to sell off the company's paper mills—a move that many considered to be reckless, since Kimberly-Clark was primarily known as a paper company. Instead, Smith focused on transforming Kimberly-Clark into a consumer paper products company. He reinvested in brands like Huggies and Kleenex, which eventually propelled the company to new heights. Smith's humility was evident in his reluctance to take credit for the company's success, even though his bold decisions were responsible for it. His quiet but relentless determination turned Kimberly-Clark into a powerhouse, outperforming competitors for decades.

On a more personal level, think about a team leader who steps up during a critical project but deflects praise to their team when the project is a success. This kind of leader doesn't need recognition because their primary goal is to see the organization or their team thrive. They build trust and loyalty because they lead with humility while remaining laser-focused on delivering exceptional results.

Building a Hedgehog Concept: Passion, Skill, and Value

Collins introduces the **Hedgehog Concept** as the intersection of three critical factors: what you are deeply passionate about, what you can be the best in the world at, and what drives your economic engine. Finding this sweet spot can elevate a good organization or leader to greatness, creating a sustainable path to success.

Imagine an entrepreneur running a mid-sized tech company. They have the passion and drive, but until they clarify their Hedgehog Concept, they're unable to scale effectively. One day, after analyzing the business's performance and customer feedback, they realize that their true strength lies not in the cutting-edge technology they've been trying to develop but in their ability to create user-friendly software that simplifies complex processes. This is what they're best at. By focusing on this Hedgehog Concept—creating intuitive, accessible software that their customers love—they align their passion, skill, and economic drivers. They begin to see sustained growth as they carve out a niche in the market where they excel.

On a larger scale, look at **Apple** during Steve Jobs' second tenure as CEO. Apple's Hedgehog Concept was clear: design beautiful, easy-to-use products that integrate seamlessly into people's lives. Jobs wasn't interested in producing a wide range of products.

Instead, he focused on a few things Apple could do better than anyone else—iPhones, iPads, and MacBooks—all of which aligned with Apple's strengths in design and innovation. By focusing on its Hedgehog Concept, Apple became a leader in consumer technology, not by being the cheapest or the most feature-heavy, but by being the best at delivering a premium user experience. This intersection of passion (design), skill (technology), and value (profitability) propelled Apple to become one of the most successful companies in the world.

The Flywheel and the Doom Loop:
Momentum vs. Stagnation

One of the most important metaphors Collins uses in **Good to Great** is that of the **Flywheel**. Imagine trying to turn a giant, heavy flywheel. At first, it takes immense effort just to get it to budge. But as you keep pushing, it gains momentum. Eventually, it begins to spin on its own, requiring less effort to maintain its speed. This is how greatness works—it's the result of consistent, focused effort over time, leading to sustained success. The flywheel is not moved by one big push but by a series of small, deliberate actions that build on each other.

An example of the Flywheel effect in action is **Amazon**. In its early years, Amazon wasn't the behemoth it is today. Founder **Jeff Bezos** started with a singular focus: selling books online. Slowly, the company expanded its offerings, improved its distribution systems, and invested heavily in customer experience. Over time, these efforts began to compound. The flywheel started spinning faster. As Amazon grew, it reinvested its profits into innovation and infrastructure, which in turn led to more customers, more revenue, and more opportunities for growth. Today, Amazon's flywheel continues to spin at breakneck speed, allowing the company to dominate e-commerce and cloud computing.

In contrast, the **Doom Loop** represents the opposite of the Flywheel. It's when organizations or leaders try to achieve greatness with quick fixes, sporadic efforts, or constantly shifting strategies. Instead of building momentum, they stagnate. One example could be a company that constantly reorganizes its structure or pivots to new markets without giving any single strategy enough time to bear fruit. Without consistency and focus, the company fails to build momentum and finds itself stuck in the Doom Loop, unable to achieve sustained success.

Consider a software company that keeps changing direction based on the latest trends rather than sticking to a well-thought-out strategy. One year, they focus on enterprise solutions; the next, they pivot to mobile apps; the following year, they switch to artificial intelligence. Instead of building momentum in any one area, they spread themselves too thin and never gain traction in any market. Their constant shifting leads to internal confusion, lost opportunities, and ultimately stagnation. They find themselves trapped in the Doom Loop, where no progress is ever sustained, and each failure leads to another shift in direction.

In contrast, another software company that focuses relentlessly on one core product—say, cloud storage—steadily improves and refines its offering. It builds partnerships, improves user experience, and gradually expands its customer base. Each small success builds on the last until the company becomes a leader in the cloud storage industry. Their flywheel gains momentum, and their success becomes self-sustaining.

To apply the Flywheel concept in your own life or leadership, think about the actions you take consistently over time. It's not the grand gestures that lead to greatness but the small, focused efforts that compound and build momentum. This could be as simple as committing to a daily habit of learning, refining a business process, or building a strong company culture. Each small step pushes the flywheel, creating sustainable growth and long-term success.

Practical Application and Final Thoughts

Whether you are a leader in a corporate environment, running a small business, or managing a team, the principles discussed in this chapter provide a roadmap for moving from good to great. Develop **Level 5 Leadership** by practicing humility and focusing on the success of your organization or team, rather than your own recognition. Identify your **Hedgehog Concept** by clarifying your passion, your strengths, and what drives your economic engine. Focus your energy on what you can do better than anyone else, and don't get distracted by opportunities that don't align with your core strengths. Finally, build momentum with the **Flywheel Effect** by taking consistent, focused actions that build on each other over time.

Greatness is not achieved overnight, nor is it the result of a single, monumental effort. It is the product of disciplined, purposeful actions that create lasting momentum. Whether you're leading a global corporation or a small team, these principles will help you move beyond mediocrity and achieve sustained success that benefits not only your organization but everyone you lead.

By applying these lessons to your own leadership journey, you can ensure that you not only achieve success in the short term but also build a foundation for greatness that endures over time.

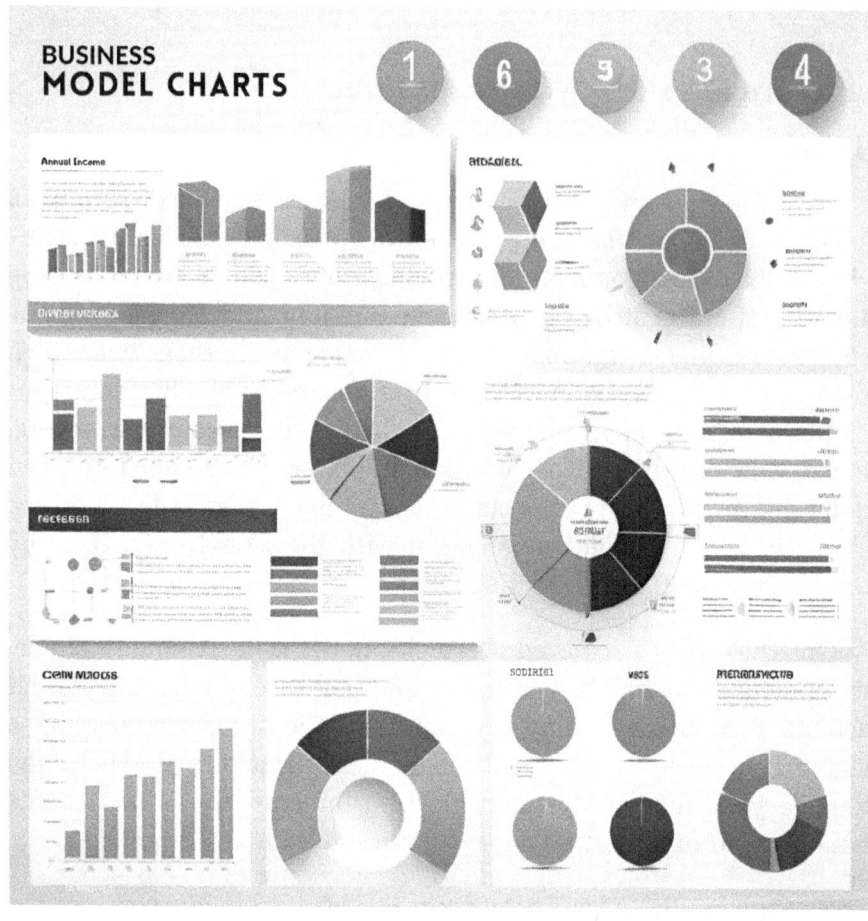

Chapter 15: Strategic Execution: Turning Plans into Action

Strategic execution is where the rubber meets the road. It's not enough to craft a brilliant strategy; the real challenge lies in effectively translating that strategy into action. This is where leaders often falter, as the gap between strategy and execution can be wide. But strategic execution is the bridge that connects lofty plans with concrete results. This chapter explores how leaders can ensure that their strategic vision becomes reality, how to adapt flexibly as circumstances change, and how to measure success while learning from failure.

Let's move deeper into these concepts by understanding what truly makes strategy work in practice.

Closing the Distance Between Strategy and Execution

One of the most common challenges for leaders is ensuring that the organization's strategy is successfully implemented across all levels. A strategy that looks great on paper can easily lose its effectiveness if not carefully executed. Why does this happen? The primary reason is the **gap between the planners and the doers**—between those who develop the strategy and those who are responsible for carrying it out.

Take, for example, **Howard Schultz** and his role in transforming Starbucks. In the early 2000s, Starbucks was growing rapidly, but Schultz noticed the company was losing its connection to the core mission that made it successful in the first place. The customer experience was beginning to suffer as the company expanded. Schultz crafted a new strategy centered around revitalizing the Starbucks culture and improving the customer experience. However, he realized that simply communicating this strategy from the top down wouldn't be enough. He made it a priority to personally engage with employees at all levels of the company, ensuring that they understood and embraced the strategic vision. He didn't just outline a plan; he created a sense of ownership across the organization. Starbucks' success wasn't the result of a strategy alone—it was because Schultz and his team successfully closed the gap between strategy and execution by embedding the new plan into the company's daily operations.

On a smaller scale, consider a local business trying to revamp its customer service. The owner creates a strategy to improve the customer experience, but if the frontline employees don't buy into the vision, the changes will never take hold. The owner must ensure that the strategy is clear, actionable, and communicated effectively to everyone involved. This means engaging employees in conversations, listening to their feedback, and showing them how their day-to-day work directly contributes to the company's success. By aligning everyone's efforts with the strategy, the business can make tangible improvements in customer satisfaction.

Continuous Adaptation and Flexibility in Leadership

No strategy survives unchanged in the face of reality. Successful leaders understand that while they must be committed to their goals, they must also be adaptable. Flexibility in leadership is about knowing when to stick with a plan and when to pivot in response to changing conditions.

One of the most vivid examples of adaptability in leadership comes from **Elon Musk**, CEO of Tesla and SpaceX. Musk is known for his ambitious goals, but what sets him apart is his ability to adapt when faced with challenges. When Tesla was struggling with production delays for the Model 3, Musk didn't abandon his strategy, but he adapted it. He personally took control of production, making significant changes to the process and even sleeping in the factory to oversee progress. This hands-on approach allowed him to diagnose bottlenecks and improve efficiency. Tesla eventually overcame its production issues, and the Model 3 went on to become one of the best-selling electric vehicles in the world.

The same principle applies to smaller organizations and teams. Consider a nonprofit that has set ambitious goals for fundraising but faces unexpected obstacles, such as economic downturns or changes in donor behavior. The leadership team needs to reassess their strategy and adapt it to the new reality. Maybe they focus more on digital fundraising or build stronger relationships with smaller donors instead of relying on a few large contributors. Adaptability doesn't mean abandoning the core mission; it means being willing to adjust tactics to stay on course toward the ultimate goal.

Flexibility is also critical in responding to **technological shifts**. As new technologies emerge, leaders must be willing to integrate them into their strategy, even if it means disrupting their current operations. The most successful leaders see these disruptions not as threats but as opportunities to innovate and evolve.

MEASURING SUCCESS AND LEARNING FROM FAILURE

A key component of strategic execution is measuring progress. This goes beyond simply tracking financial metrics; it's about understanding whether the strategy is delivering the desired outcomes and making adjustments when it's not. Leaders who excel at execution use data to inform their decisions, but they also understand that numbers alone don't tell the whole story.

"Consider the case of **Nokia**, which once dominated the mobile phone market. Despite its strong brand and innovative products, Nokia failed to adapt to the shift towards smartphones and touch-screen devices. Meanwhile, competitors like Apple and

Samsung seized the opportunity, executing a clear vision for the future of mobile technology. Apple's iPhone revolutionized the industry with its multi-touch interface and app ecosystem, while Samsung's Galaxy series offered a range of Android-based devices that appealed to a broad customer base. As a result, Nokia's leadership was left playing catch-up, unable to match the innovation and agility of its competitors. This example highlights the importance of balancing empathy, execution, and growth in leadership. If Nokia's leaders had been more attuned to customer needs and technological trends, they might have executed a more effective response to the changing market, potentially altering the company's fate."

Leaders who embrace measurement as part of their execution strategy are also more likely to learn from failure. **Failure is not the opposite of success; it's part of the journey.** Take, for example, **Jeff Bezos** and Amazon. Bezos is known for saying that Amazon's success is built on a series of failures, including high-profile flops like the Amazon Fire Phone. Instead of viewing these failures as setbacks, Bezos saw them as learning opportunities. He used the lessons from those failures to refine Amazon's strategy, which led to greater success in other areas, such as the creation of the Amazon Echo and the expansion of Amazon Web Services (AWS).

In smaller settings, imagine a startup that has launched a new product. Initial sales are disappointing, and the team might be tempted to abandon the product altogether. But if the leadership takes the time to analyze the failure—why the product didn't resonate with customers, where they might have misjudged the market—they can glean valuable insights that inform their next move. Perhaps the product was priced too high, or the marketing didn't connect with the target audience. By measuring what went wrong, the team can pivot and potentially turn the failure into a future success.

STRATEGIC EXECUTION IN PRACTICE

Bridging the gap between strategy and execution requires more than just good intentions; it requires clear communication, alignment, and relentless focus on the details that make or break a plan. Leaders must engage with every level of their organization, ensuring that the strategy is understood and embraced by those responsible for its execution. This often means going beyond memos and meetings—it means getting into the trenches and making sure that everyone, from the executives to the front-line workers, is aligned with the vision.

Flexibility is equally crucial. In today's rapidly changing environment, a rigid approach to strategy can be disastrous. Leaders must constantly monitor the external landscape, remain open to feedback, and be willing to make adjustments when necessary. Strategic execution is not a straight line; it's a winding path that requires adaptability and resilience.

Finally, leaders must embrace a culture of measurement and learning. Success and failure are both valuable teachers. By continuously measuring progress and learning from both wins and losses, leaders can ensure that their strategies not only get executed but also evolve and improve over time. This approach builds a strong foundation for sustainable growth and long-term success.

Strategic execution is where great leadership is tested. It's not enough to dream big—you have to turn those dreams into reality, one deliberate step at a time. Through discipline, adaptability, and a commitment to continuous improvement, you can bridge the gap between strategy and execution, driving your organization toward sustained success.

Dr. Jordan Dickson

Chapter 16: Leading into the Future

The most exceptional leaders are not just focused on the present—they are the ones who have the foresight to lead their organizations into the future. In today's fast-paced, rapidly changing world, it's more critical than ever to **future-proof** your strategy, adapt to technological and cultural shifts, and ultimately, leave a legacy that transcends your time at the helm. This chapter will explore what it takes to build a strategy that not only works today but is resilient enough to thrive in the years to come. We'll also consider the importance of legacy—what kind of lasting impact a leader leaves behind, both for the organization and for the people within it.

Future-Proofing Your Strategy

To future-proof your strategy means to prepare for the inevitable uncertainties that lie ahead. The world of business is full of disruptions—economic downturns, technological breakthroughs, shifts in consumer behavior, and even global crises. A future-proof strategy doesn't just react to these changes; it anticipates them.

Let's take **Satya Nadella,** the CEO of Microsoft, as an example. When he took over the company, Microsoft was lagging behind in key areas such as cloud computing, artificial intelligence, and mobile technology. Nadella recognized that to future-proof Microsoft, the company needed to pivot its strategy to focus on these emerging sectors. His vision was clear: shift the focus from Windows-centric thinking to a broader approach that embraced the cloud and AI as the future. He made strategic bets on cloud computing with Azure, and today, Azure is one of the leading cloud platforms globally, driving Microsoft's growth. Nadella's approach demonstrates that future-proofing isn't about abandoning your core; it's about evolving it to remain relevant.

For smaller businesses or even individuals in leadership positions, future-proofing can mean staying informed about industry trends, investing in continuous learning, and being open to pivoting when necessary. This might involve embracing new technology, diversifying revenue streams, or exploring partnerships that allow you to navigate the unknown with greater confidence.

Consider **Blockbuster's downfall** in contrast. Blockbuster had numerous opportunities to adapt to changing market dynamics, especially with the rise of streaming. They had the chance to buy Netflix early on, but instead, they doubled down on their brick-and-mortar business model, ultimately leading to their demise. *The lesson here is that leaders must be willing to disrupt their own strategies* before external forces do it for them.

ADAPTING TO TECHNOLOGICAL AND CULTURAL SHIFTS

One of the greatest challenges of modern leadership is adapting to the rapid pace of technological and cultural change. We live in an era where innovation is constant, and societal expectations around leadership, ethics, and corporate responsibility are evolving just as quickly.

Look at **Elon Musk** and his leadership of Tesla and SpaceX. Musk is known for his forward-thinking approach, particularly in how he leverages technology to revolutionize entire industries. From electric vehicles to reusable rockets, Musk has consistently placed his companies at the cutting edge of technological innovation. Yet, beyond the technology itself, Musk's leadership has also adapted to cultural shifts. His focus on **environmental sustainability** Tesla speaks to a growing global consciousness about climate change. His ability to align technological innovation with broader societal concerns—like sustainability—has helped him remain ahead of the curve and inspire both employees and consumers.

In a smaller business or team context, adapting to technological shifts might mean adopting new tools and platforms that make work more efficient, collaborative, or scalable. It could involve understanding the cultural shifts that impact your workforce, such as the growing demand for remote work or the increasing emphasis on diversity, equity, and inclusion. Leaders who ignore these trends risk becoming irrelevant, both in terms of attracting talent and connecting with customers.

Consider also the role of **culture in leadership. Howard Schultz** Starbucks understood that while coffee was the product, the company's culture was its most valuable asset. Schultz saw early on that Starbucks wasn't just selling coffee; it was selling an experience, a place where people could feel a sense of community. As societal norms around work-life balance, social responsibility, and ethical consumption shifted, Starbucks adapted by focusing on fair trade coffee, offering better employee benefits, and engaging in social causes. Schultz adapted Starbucks' strategy to not only meet consumer demands but also to reflect cultural values that were increasingly important to his customer base.

For leaders in any organization, the takeaway is clear: technological and cultural shifts aren't trends to be ignored—they're powerful forces that can define your leadership and the future of your organization. Understanding these shifts, and being willing to evolve in response to them, is essential for staying competitive and relevant.

Leaving a Lasting Impact: The Role of Legacy in Leadership

When we talk about leadership legacy, we're talking about the impact a leader leaves behind after they've moved on. Legacy is not just about results or financial success—it's about the imprint you leave on the people you've led, the culture you've nurtured, and the contributions you've made to your industry or society.

Consider **Steve Jobs** and the legacy he left behind at Apple. Jobs wasn't just a visionary in terms of product design—he left an enduring culture of innovation that continues to define Apple long after his passing. His emphasis on aesthetics, user experience, and simplicity still shapes the company's products today. Jobs' legacy isn't just the iPhone; it's the culture of **thinking differently** that he instilled in the company. That culture continues to drive Apple's success, even as leadership has changed.

On a more personal level, **Mother Teresa** offers a profound example of legacy beyond business. She dedicated her life to serving the poorest of the poor and left behind an extraordinary humanitarian legacy that continues to inspire millions. Her leadership wasn't measured by financial success but by the countless lives she touched, the compassion she showed, and the values she lived by. Mother Teresa's legacy teaches us that leadership isn't just about what you achieve—it's about the lives you impact along the way.

As a leader, your legacy might be the culture you build within your team, the ethical standards you uphold, or the mentorship and guidance you provide to others. It's the values you instill in your organization, which may endure long after you're gone. **Simon Sinek** talks about this in his book **Leaders Eat Last**—true leaders create environments where people feel safe, valued, and empowered to do their best work. That's the kind of legacy that transcends profit margins and quarterly reports.

In practical terms, leaving a lasting legacy means making decisions that aren't just focused on short-term gains. It involves thinking about the long-term impact of your actions—on your employees, your customers, your industry, and even society as a whole. It means being intentional about the kind of leader you want to be remembered as, and ensuring that your actions today reflect that vision.

LEADERSHIP BEYOND THE PRESENT

Leading into the future is not a passive exercise; it requires a mindset focused on resilience, adaptability, and a commitment to creating something that outlasts the present moment. Whether through future-proofing your strategy, adapting to technological and cultural changes, or shaping a meaningful legacy, your leadership has the potential to leave an indelible mark.

Great leaders understand that their influence extends far beyond their immediate role. They think not only about the results they want to achieve today but about the impact they want to have tomorrow. They understand that success isn't just measured in financial terms but in the positive change they inspire, the culture they create, and the legacy they leave behind.

Conclusion

As we reach the end of Leadership Mastery: Mastering Strategy for Visionary Mindset, it's clear that effective leadership is not confined to any single approach or quick fix. True leadership requires the cultivation of a strategic mindset—one that embraces long-term thinking, adapts to change, and balances innovation with execution. The leaders who succeed are those who constantly challenge themselves to grow, empower others, and build resilient organizations that thrive even in the face of uncertainty.

This book has provided you with the tools, insights, and real-world examples to help you master the art of strategic leadership. Whether it's fostering trust and collaboration within your team, making data-driven decisions, or navigating complex challenges with confidence, the knowledge you've gained here is meant to be a lasting guide as you continue your leadership journey.

Remember, visionary leadership is about more than achieving short-term success—it's about leaving a legacy that shapes the future. As you apply the principles from this book, take time to reflect on your purpose, inspire others, and lead with intention. You have the potential to make a lasting impact, and by mastering the strategic leadership mindset, you are already well on your way to achieving it.

Thank you for embarking on this journey, and may your leadership continue to grow, inspire, and drive the success you seek.

Appendix

Practical Tools and Worksheets for Strategic Planning

In this appendix, you'll find practical tools and worksheets designed to help you put the strategic leadership principles discussed in this book into action. These tools are meant to guide you through the processes of planning, decision-making, and execution, ensuring that your strategy is not just theoretical but actionable. Whether you're leading a team, building a business, or embarking on a personal leadership journey, these resources are adaptable to a variety of contexts.

1. Strategic Planning Worksheet

Objective: Outline your strategic goals, key initiatives, and metrics for success. This worksheet is designed to help you clarify your vision and break it down into actionable steps.

Vision Statement:

Describe your long-term vision in one sentence.

Key Objectives:

List your top 3-5 strategic objectives.

- Objective 1: _____

- Objective 2: _____

- Objective 3: _____

- **Key Initiatives:**

Identify the major projects or initiatives that will drive your objectives.

- Initiative 1: _____

- Initiative 2: _____

- Initiative 3: _____

Metrics for Success:

Define how you will measure success for each objective.

- Metric for Objective 1: _____

- Metric for Objective 2: _____

- Metric for Objective 3: _____

2. SWOT Analysis Template

Objective: Conduct a SWOT analysis to assess your organization's or team's internal strengths and weaknesses, as well as external opportunities and threats.

Strengths:

What are your organization's or team's strongest attributes? (e.g., strong culture, innovative products)

- Strength 1: _____

- Strength 2: _____

Weaknesses:

Where do you have gaps or areas for improvement? (e.g., resource constraints, skill gaps)

- Weakness 1: _____

- Weakness 2: _____

Opportunities:

What external factors or trends could benefit your organization? (e.g., market growth, emerging technologies)

- Opportunity 1: _____

- Opportunity 2: _____

Threats:

What external factors or challenges could pose a risk? (e.g., competitors, economic downturns)

- Threat 1: _____

- Threat 2: _____

3. Decision-Making Matrix

Objective: Use this matrix to evaluate potential strategic decisions based on various criteria such as cost, impact, and feasibility. This tool will help you prioritize initiatives and make informed choices.

Decision Options:

List your top decision options.

- Option 1: _____

- Option 2: _____

- Option 3: _____

Criteria:

Define the key criteria for evaluation (e.g., cost, strategic alignment, risk).

- Criteria 1: _____

- Criteria 2: _____

- Criteria 3: _____

Rating System:

Rate each option on a scale of 1-5 for each criterion.

Option	Criteria 1	Criteria 2	Criteria 3	Total Score
Option 1	___	___	___	___
Option 2	___	___	___	___
Option 3	___	___	___	___

4. Leadership Reflection Worksheet

Objective: Reflect on your leadership journey, identify areas for growth, and set personal leadership development goals.

Leadership Strengths:

What are your key leadership strengths?

- Strength 1: _____

- Strength 2: _____

Areas for Development:

Where do you see room for personal growth?

- Area 1: _____

- Area 2: _____

Action Plan:

What actions will you take to grow in these areas?

- Action 1: _____

- Action 2: _____

- **Support Needed:**

Who or what resources can support you in your growth?

- Support 1: _____

- Support 2: _____

5. Scenario Planning Worksheet

Objective: Plan for various future scenarios to ensure your strategy is resilient to changes in the environment.

Scenario 1:

Describe the best-case scenario for your strategy.

- Key Assumptions: _____

- Strategic Response: _____

Scenario 2:

Describe the worst-case scenario.

- Key Assumptions: _____

- Strategic Response: _____

- **Scenario 3:**

Describe the most likely scenario.

- Key Assumptions: _____

- Strategic Response: _____

Illustrations

1. Vision-Action Alignment

(Visual representation of how vision, objectives, and initiatives align to drive success.)

Example: An illustration showing a leader standing at the intersection of vision and action, with arrows pointing towards key initiatives and outcomes.

2. SWOT Analysis Diagram

(A quadrant diagram illustrating the strengths, weaknesses, opportunities, and threats.)

Example: A box divided into four quadrants, each labeled with S (Strengths), W (Weaknesses), O (Opportunities), and T (Threats), filled with sample responses.

3. Decision Matrix Chart

(Visual representation of a decision matrix with various options plotted according to criteria scores.)

Example: A chart showing different strategic decisions mapped out based on feasibility and impact scores.

These tools are meant to serve as a bridge between the concepts of strategic leadership and their practical application, making it easier to implement the strategies discussed throughout the book.

Self-Reflection Questions for Personal Development

Self-reflection is a powerful tool for personal growth and leadership development. The following questions are designed to help you gain deeper insights into your leadership style, mindset, and personal values. Take some time to ponder these questions, and consider journaling your answers as you reflect on your leadership journey.

Leadership Mindset

- What are the core values that drive my leadership decisions?

- How do I define success as a leader, beyond just financial metrics?

- In what ways do I exhibit resilience when faced with setbacks or challenges?

- Am I creating an environment where my team feels empowered and supported? How could I improve in this area?

Personal Growth

- How do I handle uncertainty or ambiguity in my leadership role?

- What have been my biggest leadership lessons to date? How have they shaped me?

- Am I taking enough time for self-care and renewal to ensure I'm leading at my best?

- What steps can I take to become more adaptable and open to change?

Purpose and Impact

- Am I leading with a sense of purpose that extends beyond profit? What is my "why" as a leader?

- How can I ensure that my leadership has a positive and lasting impact on my team, organization, or community?

- How do I measure the legacy I want to leave as a leader? What actions am I taking today to build that legacy?

Relationships and Collaboration

- How do I foster trust and collaboration among my team members?

- In what ways do I show vulnerability in leadership to build stronger connections with my team?

- How can I manage team conflict? Am I creating an environment where healthy conflict is encouraged?

Further Reading on Leadership, Strategy, and Innovation

For those who want to deepen their understanding of strategic leadership and innovation, here is a list of recommended readings that provide valuable insights, frameworks, and case studies. These books and articles expand on the themes covered in this book and offer additional tools to help you grow as a leader.

Leadership and Personal Development

"Brené Brown, "The Gifts of Imperfection"

This book explores vulnerability, courage, and the power of embracing imperfections as a leader. Brown's research into human connection and resilience is both inspiring and practical for personal growth.

"Viktor E. Frankl's "Man's Search for Meaning"

A deeply philosophical reflection on finding purpose through suffering, this classic text offers profound lessons on leading with a sense of mission and leaving a meaningful impact.

"The 7 Habits of Highly Effective People" by Stephen Covey

Covey's principles for personal and professional effectiveness are foundational for any leader seeking to cultivate discipline, integrity, and influence.

Strategy and Innovation

"Good Strategy, Bad Strategy" by Richard Rumelt

Rumelt provides a clear distinction between effective and ineffective strategies, offering insights into diagnosing challenges and creating actionable, coherent plans.

- *"Blue Ocean Strategy" by W. Chan Kim and Renée Mauborgne*

This book introduces the concept of creating uncontested market spaces where competition is irrelevant, and it offers practical advice for breaking out of saturated markets.

- *"The Innovator's Dilemma"* by Clayton Christensen

Christensen's groundbreaking work explores why successful companies often fail in the face of disruptive innovation and how leaders can prepare for and navigate these changes.

Organizational Leadership and Team Dynamics

- *"Leaders Eat Last" by Simon Sinek*

This book delves into the importance of creating environments of trust and safety within teams, demonstrating how servant leadership can drive long-term success.

- *"The Five Dysfunctions of a Team" by Patrick Lencioni*

Lencioni offers an insightful look into the common pitfalls of teamwork and how leaders can overcome these challenges to create more cohesive and effective teams.

- *"Drive: The Surprising Truth About What Motivates Us" by Daniel H. Pink*

Pink explores the science of motivation, revealing how autonomy, mastery, and purpose can inspire greater performance and satisfaction in teams.

These resources offer a well-rounded exploration of leadership, strategy, and innovation. Together with the principles and strategies discussed in this book, they can serve as an invaluable foundation for your ongoing journey toward becoming an impactful and strategic leader.

ABOUT THE AUTHOR

Jordan Dickson is an accomplished leadership strategist and executive coach with a passion for helping leaders unlock their full potential. With a career spanning over two decades, Jordan has guided leaders at every level—from CEOs of Fortune 500 companies to entrepreneurs at innovative startups. His expertise lies in crafting strategic solutions that balance visionary thinking with practical execution, enabling organizations to achieve sustainable success.

Jordan's approach to leadership is deeply rooted in real-world experience. He has worked alongside top executives, helping them navigate complex challenges, cultivate resilient teams, and drive growth in dynamic markets. Known for his ability to translate big-picture strategy into actionable steps, Jordan has earned a reputation as a trusted advisor who empowers leaders to think differently, inspire others, and leave a lasting impact.

In Strategic Leadership Mindset: How Visionary Leaders Master Strategy for Lasting Success, Jordan distills his extensive experience into a powerful guide designed to help readers embrace strategic thinking, foster innovation, and lead with purpose. His work is driven by the belief that great leaders are made through intentional practice, continuous learning, and a commitment to shaping a better future. Jordan Dickson's mission is to inspire the next generation of leaders to not only achieve success but to create legacies that stand the test of time.

Dr. Jordan Dickson

Dear Reader,

Thank you for taking the time to read Leadership Mastery: Mastering Strategy for Visionary Mindset. Your support means the world to me, and I hope the insights and strategies shared within these pages have inspired and empowered you on your leadership journey.

If this book has made a positive impact on you, I would greatly appreciate it if you could take a moment to leave an honest review. Your feedback helps me continue to grow as an author and allows future readers to discover how this book could help them as well. Whether it's a quick comment or a detailed reflection, every review makes a difference.

Thank you for being part of this journey, and for helping me reach more leaders like you.

With gratitude,

- Jordan Dickson

INDEX

- Accountability - 23, 25, 44, 80, 81, 83 ,89

- Apple - 8,44,45,69,76,88

- Autonomy - 29,30,69,100

- Balance - 7, 43, 65, 69, 87

- Brand Loyalty - 15,

- Cirque du Soleil - 15, 46

- Commitment - 4, 17,21, 26, 48, 60, 63, 67, 69, 72, 83, 89

- Communication -23, 66, 70, 82

- Compassion - 52, 68, 88

- Competitive Advantage - 13, 15, 17

- Continuous Growth - 29, 31, 33

- Courage - 15, 52,

- Customer Experience - 41, 44, 48, 75, 79

- Data-Driven Leadership - 41, 42, 43, 44

- Decision-Making - 10, 24, 35, 36, 43, 93

- Deep Blue Strategy - 15,

- Differentiation - 15, 36, 47

- Diversity - 21, 87

- Empathy - 19, 53, 65, 70

- Ethical Leadership - 21, 22

- Execution - 22, 37, 65, 67, 79, 81, 83

- Feedback - 23, 42, 67, 74,80, 102

- Five Forces - 13, 16, 37

- Flywheel Effect - 75, 77

- Google - 30, 41

- Growth Mindset - 21, 31, 55, 58

- Innovation - 11, 15, 25, 32, 48, 65, 99

- Leadership - 1, 19, 25, 41, 52, 59, 63, 65, 80, 89

- Legacy - 62, 69, 87,

- Michael (CEO) - 55, 67

- Mission - 24, 61, 79

- Netflix - 14, 36, 46, 86

- Opportunity - 8, 49, 68, 93

- Passion - 74, 77, 102

- Purpose - 1, 5, 31, 63, 72, 97

- Resilience - 51, 54, 89, 99

- Risk Management - 25

- Scaling Success - 47, 66, 85

- Servant Leadership - 19, 22, 100

- SpaceX - 10, 61, 66, 80, 86

- Strategic Planning - 48, 91

- Strategy -13, 16, 35, 37, 65, 79, 85

- Synergy - 23, 26

- Trust - 19, 23,

- Visionary Leadership - 3, 90

- Vulnerability - 20, 23, 51, 98

.

www.ingramcontent.com/pod-product-compliance
Lightning Source LLC
Chambersburg PA
CBHW050315230526
45471CB00005B/2200